Corruption – the World's Big C

Cases, Causes, Consequences, Cures

IAN SENIOR

The Institute of Economic Affairs

First published in Great Britain in 2006 by
The Institute of Economic Affairs
2 Lord North Street
Westminster
London SW1P 3LB
in association with Profile Books Ltd

The mission of the Institute of Economic Affairs is to improve public
understanding of the fundamental institutions of a free society, with particular
reference to the role of markets in solving economic and social problems.

A CIP catalogue record for this book is available from the British Library.

ISBN-10: 0 255 36571 3
ISBN-13: 978 0 255 36571 0

Many IEA publications are translated into languages other than English or
are reprinted. Permission to translate or to reprint should be sought from the
Director General at the address above.

Typeset in Stone by MacGuru Ltd
info@macguru.org.uk

Printed and bound in Great Britain by Hobbs the Printers

CONTENTS

Corruption – the World's Big C

Cases, Causes, Consequences, Cures

THE AUTHOR

Ian Senior was born in 1938. He was educated at the Dragon School, Oxford; Sedbergh School, Cumbria; Trinity College, Oxford, and at University College London, where he took an MSc(econ). He has been an economic consultant for over 30 years, latterly with the London office of National Economic Research Associates (NERA) and now with Triangle Management Services.

In 1970 the IEA published his ground-breaking study *The Postal Service: Competition or Monopoly?*, which long before its time argued the case for abolishing the then Post Office's monopoly of letters. Thirty-six years later, on 1 January 2006, the letter monopoly was ended in the UK, having already been abolished in the 1990s in Sweden and New Zealand. Since 1970 Ian Senior has published many articles and worked on varied consultancy assignments relating to the economics of postal services.

In the 1990s he published an extensive number of articles about the economics of the pharmaceutical industry, notably parallel trade. More recently he has written in *Economic Affairs* and elsewhere about the economics of corruption and about the financial impact of theatre criticism on the West End.

FOREWORD

In recent debates about reducing poverty in Africa liberal economists frequently opposed those who believed in greater official aid and debt reduction on the grounds that these measures did not address the cause of poverty. Furthermore, as one of the causes of poverty was corruption and corruption is generally to be found in institutions of government, any policies that increase the resources that are controlled directly by corrupt governments have the potential to increase rather than to decrease poverty.

This is a specific and important example of a general point. Corruption can seriously undermine the operation of markets wherever it is found. There is a straightforward economic transaction cost that arises from private sector agents having to make what are, in effect, transfer payments to state functionaries. But, also, prices become distorted. Competition and market entry can be impeded – particularly market entry by those whose integrity leads them to reject a culture of corruption. More seriously, a market economy can become shaken at its foundations by corruption: a corrupt government, police force or judiciary that does not enforce contracts or property rights can prevent market exchange from getting off the ground. Thus an understanding of corruption is important for understanding how market economies can develop and prosper.

We might expect that the relationship between corruption

and a market economy should work in the other direction too. Most corruption involves agents seeking favours from public officials. The larger the realm of government, the greater the opportunity for such favours to be granted. If the government regulates trade, then corruption can play a part in allocating export or import quotas. If the government does not regulate trade there are no such opportunities for preferment. If local government allocates housing using administrative criteria, opportunities for corruption are plentiful. If local government has nothing to do with the allocation of housing, opportunities for corruption are reduced. There are many more such examples … But, as the author makes clear, there is further work to be done in researching this issue. Certain enduring values seem to be more important than the amount of government intervention in determining the level of corruption (most notably personal honesty). What are we to make of the fact that there are some relatively uncorrupt countries with very intrusive governments, such as in Scandinavia? The relationship between the size of government and the amount of corruption is an important area for further research identified in this monograph. Can we create a virtuous chain of events with less government leading to less corruption and then to a better functioning of the expanded domain of the market economy?

In the absence of conclusive proof that less government is a policy that will lead to less corruption, the author proposes a 'zero tolerance' approach to corruption. He recognises that corruption will be difficult to cure. Those who are in a position to do something about corruption are the very people who benefit from it most. With regard to countries to which Britain and others give foreign aid, Ian Senior proposes that no such aid should be given without a thorough audit of financial systems and that aid should be contingent upon absence of corruption.

The author defines his terms carefully. He then applies his definition to the institutions of government around the world and finds that corruption is all too widespread. The consequences of corruption are clear: the poorer functioning of markets. Ian Senior makes a convincing case that liberal economists should be concerned by the causes and consequences of and cures for corruption.

The views expressed in this Research Monograph are, as in all IEA publications, those of the author and not those of the Institute (which has no corporate view), its managing trustees, Academic Advisory Council members or senior staff.

PHILIP BOOTH

Editorial and Programme Director,
Institute of Economic Affairs
Professor of Insurance and Risk Management,
Sir John Cass Business School, City University
May 2006

Editorial note: New cases of possible corruption come to light with great frequency. No cases have been considered for this monograph after 15 March 2006.

SUMMARY

- Economic corruption harms nations, institutions and society in much the same way that cancer harms human bodies. They both merit the sobriquet 'The Big C'.
- A robust definition of economic corruption is essential and has been lacking in previous writings. The author provides a new definition that is based on five conditions that must be satisfied simultaneously. His definition is independent of laws, ethics, customs or time and applies to all institutions in the public and private sectors everywhere.
- Corruption occurs when a corruptor covertly gives a favour to a corruptee or to a nominee to influence action(s) that may benefit the corruptor or a nominee and for which the corruptee has authority.
- A review of corruption in the UN secretariat, the European Commission, the EU-15 and some industrialised countries produces a comparative table. Medals are awarded according to the level in the hierarchy at which corruption has occurred in the last 25 years. The medals table excludes those continents, regions and many countries where corruption is so endemic as to make a medals count difficult or meaningless. The medals table is headed by France, Japan, Italy, Germany and Belgium.

- Using regression analysis and taking Transparency International's Corruption Perceptions Index 2004 as the dependent variable, the author tests fourteen independent variables for statistical significance as possible causes of corruption. Those that proved significant are: the prevalence of informal markets (more informal markets, more corruption); the respect for property rights (less respect, more corruption); the amount of regulation (more regulation, more corruption); press freedom (less freedom, more corruption); personal honesty (less honesty, more corruption); and religiosity (perhaps counter-intuitively, more church attendance being related to more corruption). A separate test showed a significant correlation between high corruption and low incomes per head.

- The consequences of corruption are shown to be: price distortion occurs even when markets appear to clear; a covert, upward redistribution of wealth within society takes place; democratic processes are subverted; financial and commercial risks are increased, affecting the willingness to invest; and society's morality and ethics decline.

- The author estimates that enlarging the EU from fifteen to 25 states has increased the overall level of corruption in the EU by nearly 5 per cent and that enlarging it further with four candidate states that include Turkey and Romania will increase the overall level of corruption by more than 10 per cent.

- The author recommends ways to tackle corruption worldwide based on two key concepts: transparency and zero tolerance. As an immediate step all multinational and unilateral aid to countries that are corrupt and that are not taking measures to root out corruption should cease.

TABLES, BOXES AND FIGURES

Corruption – the World's Big C

Cases, Causes, Consequences, Cures

1 FUNDAMENTALS

I expect that most readers are against crime and think that corruption should be classed as a crime. The problem with crime, corruption and various other acts, however, is that criminality frequently is in the eye of the beholder. Further, I am aware that some economists and others have argued that corruption is a form of oil that makes creaking government machines work better than otherwise. Later, I provide arguments and practical cases that show corruption to be a significant disbenefit to the countries where it is prevalent, but I accept that corruption, if it has not been carefully defined, is still too often a matter of personal judgement.

I am also aware that crimes of many kinds have those who defend or even justify them. In the UK most of us would describe Saddam Hussein's actions as criminal: the torturing to death of opponents, the elimination of opponents' families, the experimental destruction of a complete village to test his chemical weapons, the gassing of the Marshland Arabs and so on. But many in Iraq and in the region appear to consider these acts to be no more than realpolitik. Further, some of the actions that were commonplace under Saddam's regime were not unlike Christian practices in Europe for several centuries. Torture and execution of political opponents were routine and burning people to death for heresy was considered to be a virtuous way of saving their souls.

Not long ago the late Pope John Paul II admitted that he regretted the methods used by the Inquisition.

Fast-forward to the UK in the 1950s before the Wolfenden report. Homosexual relationships between men was a criminal offence. Sexual relationships between women were not criminal, however, because Queen Victoria believed they were impossible and none of her ministers wished to tell her otherwise

From these examples it can be seen that even if we are against crime in general and corruption in particular, there are likely to be wide variations between regions, countries, religions and ethnic groups both now and through time about what constitutes corruption and the extent to which the law should punish it. Clearly, if we are all against 'corruption' but do not define it precisely we cannot begin to analyse its causes and effects, let alone try to do something about it.

Is corruption, however defined, undesirable? A car without oil grinds to a halt within minutes. By analogy, some assert that corruption, particularly in developing countries, benefits the economy by making it work better rather than worse. For example, Theobald (1999) has argued that corruption doesn't matter very much anyway. His title encapsulates his view: 'So what really is the problem about corruption?' His conclusion is that 'not only is the underpinning dichotomy merely descriptive and therefore analytically unproductive, but the consequent policy implications [relating to corruption] may be both misplaced and inappropriate'. Seemingly corruption should be viewed as a storm in a teacup.

I reject this view. Indeed, I argue that, irrespective of the ethics and laws in any jurisdiction, corruption is economically undesirable wherever it exists: in any state, company or institution, including those in the private sector, both for-profit and not-for-profit. I maintain that this applies equally in successful, industrialised countries and in those that are developing and poor. In this context I am supported by Kaufmann and Wei (1999), who found empirical evidence that firms which bribe bureaucrats spend more, not less, management time dealing with bureaucrats and face a higher, not lower, cost of capital.

I start from the belief that corruption is a cancer. Cancer destroys individual bodies; corruption destroys institutions and societies. However, cancer spreads within a physical body but, not being contagious or infectious, remains within the body, corruption, by contrast, is both contagious and infectious. Unchecked and unpunished it can and does spread to other institutions and to other countries.

Accepting this important difference between cancer and corruption, it seems apt to refer to both as 'The Big C'. My belief is that just as doctors and scientists are continually finding ways to eliminate cancer within the human body, so politicians and heads of all forms of institutions should and could apply ways to eliminate the cancer of corruption from the institutional bodies over which they exert authority.

Defining corruption
Definitions in the literature

Readers who turn to *The Concise Oxford Dictionary* for a definition of corruption will find: 'decomposition; moral deterioration; use of corrupt practices (bribery etc.); perversion (of language etc.) from its original state'. Here I am concerned only with corruption in an economic sense and I leave moral matters to theologians, philosophers and religious teachers. My starting point is that a clear definition of corruption is essential before a discussion of the economics of corruption can take place. Only in the light of a clear definition can the laws of any country and the internal rules of public and private institutions, including companies, be formulated. Once a clear definition has been set, the actions of individuals and institutions can be judged as corrupt or uncorrupt because an accepted yardstick can be applied.

Many papers about corruption have been published in academic journals over the past 40 years, particularly in the 1990s and onwards. A selection of 113 has been republished by Williams et al. (2000) in *The Politics of Corruption*. The first volume is entitled 'Explaining Corruption'.

It would seem essential that authors who wish to write about corruption should define corruption early in their papers, either stating their own definition or drawing on those definitions already in the literature. How can you construct academic arguments if it is unclear what you are writing about? In fact, of 28 papers in the first volume only ten specifically define corruption or take an earlier definition as their starting point. A small number of definitions are succinct and are based on Waterbury (1973): corruption is 'the abuse of public power and influence for private ends'. An earlier and commonly quoted definition by Nye (1967) has the same main concept but is far more detailed: 'Corruption is behaviour which deviates from the formal duties of a public role because of private-regarding (personal, close family, private clique) pecuniary or status gains; or violates rules against the exercise of certain types of private-regarding influence.'

A later and fundamentally different definition is offered by

Alam (1989) based on the relationship between principals and their agents. He states: 'Corruption ... may be defined as (1) the sacrifice of the principal's interest for the agent's, or (2) the violation of norms defining the agent's behaviour.' A draft Corruption Bill published by the government in 2003 uses the agent/principal relationship as key to defining corruption and is therefore based on Alam's principle. A joint committee that considered the draft Bill prefers a wider definition that is closer to mine, set out below. At the time of writing, the Bill had not made a start in its passage through Parliament.

The various definitions that follow the concepts of both Waterbury and Nye all have flaws. The main weakness with Nye-type definitions is that they restrict corruption to the abuse of *public* power for *private* ends. While it is clear that corruption can frequently be traced to the interaction between functionaries who have, say, licences to award and private individuals or firms wishing to receive those licences, it is evident that corruption can and does occur also within the private, non-governmental sector. For example, the employee of a large firm who is responsible for awarding contracts may take a bribe as readily as a government functionary. Many years ago, as an economic consultant working on a project for Kellogg's cornflakes, I received a circular from the company at Christmas specifically instructing all the firm's suppliers not to give presents or to treat members of Kellogg's staff in any way.

As a further example, a parent may pay an admissions tutor a covert bribe in return for admission of their son or daughter to a university. This is potentially corrupt whether the institution concerned is fully private, fully government-owned or controlled or some hybrid of private and government-controlled, as in the

UK. It does not make sense to describe this action if it were to happen at London University as corrupt yet uncorrupt if it were to happen at Buckingham University.

The second weakness of Nye-type definitions is their reference to rules that prevail *at the time*. Laws, regulations and rules vary considerably from country to country and, within particular countries, from one period of time to another. Further, laws, regulations and rules represent what has been codified in each country and how they can be enforced if they are broken. The literature abounds with examples of countries, notably in Africa, where actions that in European countries would be seen as illegal and corrupt are considered to be normal and acceptable.

The fundamental flaw in Alam-type definitions is the concept of corruption being directly related to the relationship between principals and their agents. Alam's definition would be equally applicable to an agent who simply went to sleep during the afternoons, thus 'sacrificing his principal's interests ... and violating norms defining the agent's behaviour'. Yet nobody would describe laziness of this sort as corruption.

Among the 28 papers in the first volume of Williams et al. (2000), the wooden spoon must go to those authors who avoid settling for any definition of corruption. Foremost among these is Williams himself, who contributes two papers to the volume. In Williams (1976) he begins his paper with: 'Corruption, like beauty, is in the eye of the beholder.' Two paragraphs later he amplifies this view: 'While it is not necessary at this stage to examine any particular definition, it is important to note that there are nearly as many definitions of corruption as there are species of tropical plants and they vary as much in their appearance, character and resilience. The point is that the search for the true definition of corruption is, like the pursuit of the Holy Grail, endless, exhausting and ultimately futile.'

Williams's contention that there are nearly as many definitions of corruption as there are species of tropical plants represents surprisingly unacademic hyperbole and is far from the truth. As noted, there are few definitions and broadly they can be grouped under the headings of those of Nye or Alam. Further, to describe the attempts of various scholars to define corruption as 'endless, exhausting and ultimately futile' is to throw in the sponge at the start.

In his second paper in Williams et al. (2000), namely Williams (1999), his view of the impossibility of defining corruption has not changed in 23 years, despite his being the main editor of a four-volume work with 113 articles and 2,340 pages on the subject. He points out that 'There has been an explosion of interest in corruption in the past 10 years and the literature … is now substantial. But there has not been a corresponding concern with the concept of corruption and how it can be defined and refined … [This paper] concludes that the new concepts are attempts to explain the circumstances most likely to give rise to corruption rather than original ways of defining it.' Again he offers no definition of corruption in his paper despite the availability of several definitions within the volume, but admits that 'It is a curious state of affairs when an academic mini-industry and the policy agendas of development professionals are dominated by a concept which most participants in the debate are reluctant or unable to define.'

I agree.

Shades of corruption

An extension of the failure of many writers to put forward a convincing definition of corruption is found in Heidenheimer (1989). He classifies corruption in the following three categories as cited by Kalchheim (2004):

- 'black corruption' indicates that a particular action is one that a majority consensus of both elite and mass opinion would condemn and would want to see punished on grounds of principle;
- 'grey corruption' indicates that some elements, usually elites, may want to see the action punished, others not, and the majority may well be ambiguous;
- 'white corruption' signifies that the majority of both elite and mass opinion probably would not vigorously support an attempt to punish a form of corruption that they regard as tolerable.

It is hard to imagine a less workable set of definitions in which public opinion has to be polled on whether a given act is corrupt or not and which classifies public opinion on whether punishment is warranted into 'elite' and 'mass' opinion.

Two recent definitions

To show how some scholars are still seeking the Holy Grail, a more recent definition of corruption is found in Neild (2002): 'the breaking by public persons, for the sake of private financial or political gain, of the rules of conduct in public affairs prevailing in a society in the period under consideration'. Neild's definition is clearly part of the Nye concept with its resulting weaknesses. The definition applies solely to the public sector. Very much later, in Appendix A of his book, Neild recognises that private sector corruption is also a reality, and he extends his definition: 'When we talk of private corruption we mean dishonesty between private persons in economic transactions.'

Some examples he gives of private corruption are: 'The overcharging of customers with respect to the quantity or quality of goods or services' and 'the under-paying of suppliers'.

Neild's definitions have the merit of including 'private corruption' as occurring outside the nexus between governments and the private sector. His examples are, however, wide of the mark. The concept of 'overcharging' comes curiously from an economist since markets determine the price charged for goods and services. Further, if a supplier contracts with his customer to supply ten units and supplies only nine, the customer can take legal action to recover the final unit. If, conversely, the customer receives ten units and sends a cheque for nine, the supplier similarly can take action. Corruption occurs only if, say, the supplier charges for ten units, supplies nine and then shares the proceeds of the remaining unit with the customer, who accepts money or another favour as a reward for overlooking the fact that his firm has been defrauded.

Neild's definitions illustrate the point that any economic or social treatise that fails to define corruption tightly and convincingly at the outset lacks a framework within which to judge examples of corrupt behaviour, whether theoretical or empirical, that are then described. In essence, a clear, cogent definition of corruption is the essential starting point for all analysis. Any paper or book that does not state its definition of corruption in the first chapter is flawed.

Johnson and Sharma (2004) provide a list of forms that corruption can take which, in their view, encompass more than bribery.

1   *bribery and graft* (extortion and kickbacks);
2   *kleptocracy* (stealing and privatising public funds);
3   *misappropriation* (forgery, embezzlement, misuse of public funds);
4   *non-performance of duties* (cronyism);
5   *influence-peddling* (favour-brokering and conflict of interest);
6   *acceptance of improper gifts* ('speed' money);
7   *protecting maladministration* (cover-ups, perjury);
8   *abuse of power* (intimidation and torture);
9   *manipulation of regulations* (bias and election rigging);
10 *electoral malpractice* (vote buying and election rigging);
11 *rent-seeking* (public officials who illegally charge for services after creating an artificial shortage);
12 *clientelism and patronage* (politicians giving material favours in exchange for citizen support);
13 *illegal campaign contributions* (giving unregulated gifts to influence policies and regulations).

Casual readers going through this list would be forgiven for thinking it rather widespread but might accept it by and large as describing or categorising forms of corruption. Some aspects seem, however, to have overstepped even a layman's reasonable definitions. For example, if kleptocracy is defined as stealing public funds this must include social security fraud, which extends the definition of corruption to a point where it ceases to be useful. Similarly, to describe torture as a form of corruption is clearly unhelpful because it is unclear who is the corruptor and who the corruptee. Further, torture falls into the realm of morality, not economics.

The fundamental weakness of this list is that it *describes* what may be corrupt practices but it does not *define* the concept itself.

The author's definition

I now put forward my definition of corruption. Before being published in Senior (1998) the definition was commented on by at least six economists who were my colleagues when I worked in the London office of National Economic Research Associates (NERA). It was discussed in an internal seminar in NERA and again in 2003 at an IEA seminar; and it was published with one change in Senior (2004). I would not describe it necessarily as the 'Holy Grail', but it has clear benefits compared with the definitions cited earlier. I offer it as a basis for discussion in further academic papers and, more importantly, by those concerned in the legislature, the judiciary and in management at all levels in any form of institution who wish to confront corruption and take action against it.

The definition consists of five conditions that *must all be satisfied simultaneously*. Corruption occurs when a corruptor (1) *covertly* gives (2) *a favour* to a corruptee or to a nominee to influence (3) *action(s)* that (4) *benefit* the corruptor or a nominee, and for which the corruptee has (5) *authority*.

The favour must be a positive good or service such as money or a free holiday. Negative goods or services such as physical violence or blackmail cannot be described as favours and so are excluded.

Condition (4) might seem superfluous. Why should a corruptor bother to give a favour if he or a nominee is not to benefit in some way? It has been pointed out, however, that without Condition (4) anonymous gifts to charity could be classified as corruption. Suppose I anonymously (*covertly*) give £1 million (*a favour*) to a cancer foundation that influences the *actions* for which the research foundation has *authority*. Lacking Condition (4), the gift under my definition could be classified as corruption even if few would regard it as such.

When Condition 4 is added, because the anonymous donor does not receive a benefit, the gift is not corrupt. Even if the anonymous donor stipulated specific nominees such as particular African states, his anonymity would ensure that neither the African states nor the cancer foundation would be able to favour him in any way, so he receives nothing but a feel-good factor, which cannot be considered as a favour.

If Condition (4) is included I, the anonymous donor, may ultimately benefit if I am a cancer sufferer. Suppose by chance the institution spends my anonymous (*covert*) donation on my sort of cancer and five years later produces a new treatment that benefits me personally; in this case my covert donation retrospectively appears to become corruption. It seems clear that this example is so far fetched as to be trivial, but I include Condition (4) in the definition so that the latter is as robust as possible.

The use of my definition has many advantages:

- it is succinct and transparent;
- it distinguishes corruption from crime in general and from fraud and theft in particular, as will be discussed below;
- it is applicable to actions that take place at any level in any institution within any sector – public, private, voluntary and charitable;
- it is independent of time;

- it is independent of the country or jurisdiction in which actions occur;
- it is independent of moral judgements; and
- it is independent of both the laws and the customs in the jurisdictions or institutions concerned.

A question arises if someone gives a covert favour to an individual or to an organisation with the intention of receiving a favour such as a contract or a peerage but the hoped-for actions on the part of the recipient do not happen. Under my definition, corruption has *not* occurred because the would-be corruptor has parted with money but received nothing in return. For corruption to occur, it must be shown that the *covert favour* did indeed *influence actions* over which the corruptee has *authority*.

This case nicely distinguishes between the *intent to corrupt* and, for example, the *intent* to burgle. A burglar caught with a jemmy outside the window of a house can be fined or jailed for his intent. By contrast, a covert political donation that provenly does not influence the recipient is not corrupt, even if its intent was corrupt. In this context the need for political donations above a certain size to be *overt* by being declared to an electoral commission or included by the recipient in a public register of interests is a powerful tool to prevent premeditated corruption. This is discussed later.

Within the advantages of my definition, the last has particular strength. Changes in criminal laws generally follow changes in opinion or social developments, sometimes with a delay of many years. For example, since the 1950s Oscar Wilde would not have been imprisoned for his relationship with Lord Alfred Douglas, though he would still be imprisoned for those with partners who were under sixteen. The age of male consent was reduced from eighteen to sixteen recently. Who knows what age of consent may be legalised in the future?

Distinction between corruption and theft

Differentiating corruption from theft is important. In theft there are *two* parties: one steals and the other is stolen from. A corrupt person may steal from individuals or from groups including the state but theft is distinct from corruption because under my definition of corruption *three parties are involved*: the corruptor, the corruptee and those others who are directly influenced for better or worse by the actions taken by the corruptee. They are beneficiaries or victims.

At an individual level, if a thief takes £10 from my wallet, he is better off and I am worse off. Nobody else is affected.

With corruption, more than two parties are involved. For example, if a corrupt contractor bribes an official to award his firm a contract there is a direct impact on the firm that wins the project and on those firms that failed to win it. Let us further assume that the winning contractor offered a bribe to a functionary to accept his higher-priced bid. There is now also an indirect impact on those who pay for the project, typically taxpayers. Some part of the full cost of the project has gone into the bank account of the functionary concerned. Taxpayers receive a finished hospital, let us say, but they pay more for it than they would have paid under an uncorrupt tendering system. Alternatively, for a given price they receive a sub-standard hospital because the corrupt contractor has to recoup the cost of the bribe.

By contrast, if a thief steals a contractor's lorry, it is clear that the contractor is the poorer and the thief is the richer, but it does not follow that third parties suffer.

Another form of theft is mentioned in the literature: klepto-cracy, meaning government by thieves. This was the state of affairs in Nigeria (described later) and in the failed bank, BCCI. In both cases those at the top had direct access to national or corporate assets. They did not need to rely on bribes from corruptors: they simply drew on national or corporate assets in favour of them-selves. This is theft on a grand scale and, though it may occur at the same time as corruption, it remains distinct from the latter.

Fraud

Fraud can be thought of as a sub-set of theft. A person who defrauds another individual or organisation takes assets to which he has no title. There is little practical difference between theft and fraud except that theft commonly refers to taking physical assets. Only recently has 'identity theft' become an issue. Identity theft may result in a false passport that permits illegal travel across frontiers or illegal work within a jurisdiction. More commonly, however, identity theft leads to monetary theft in the form of using a credit card or emptying the victim's bank account.

Fraud, on the other hand, normally entails the application of false information. At one end of the scale, charging expenses of £10 for a £5 taxi trip is fraud. In the middle of the scale, tax evasion is fraud. At a higher level, an EU case came to light of Greek importers claiming subsidies for sugar cane supposedly grown in Croatia. The fraud continued for several years because the European Commission's functionaries supposedly had not noticed that Croatia's climate does not permit growing sugar cane.

While none of these cases of fraud constitutes corruption as I have defined it, they suggest a climate in which fraud and corruption may happily coexist.

Theft, fraud and corruption compared

Does it matter if a given action is classified as theft, fraud or corruption? I suggest it does. Consider that you lose £1,000 through theft, fraud or corruption. All other factors are held constant: for example, no violence is involved. Would you be indifferent as to how the loss occurred?

Theft has been part of society through time, but if a jurisdiction has established property rights, a competent police force and an honest legal system, your £1,000 may be restored to you if the thief is found while still in possession of your money.

Fraud is a more sophisticated form of theft. Suppose that you lose £1,000 because you are advised by a confidence trickster to invest in a non-existent company. You will certainly feel aggrieved but you will hope for restitution if the trickster is brought to justice.

But if you know that the thief or the trickster will not be brought to justice because he can bribe the police or the judge or both, your frustration, I suggest, will be more intense. If so, corruption is more damaging to the structure of society than theft or fraud. Furthermore, corruption is *covert*, and third parties suffer. Those who suffer from corruption may suffer grievously but never be able to identify the cause of their suffering – and thus never receive restitution.

Insider dealing

Under the terms of the Companies Act it is illegal for anyone to use 'inside' information about a company to profit from buying or selling its shares. People are 'insiders' if they have access to information that has not been made available to all investors.

Taking the example of publicly quoted shares, typically prior knowledge of (say) a pending takeover gives an opportunity to buy shares in the target company before the news is public and to realise a quick gain when the bid increases the value of the target company's shares. Stock exchanges, financial regulators and quoted companies lay down rules that are aimed at preventing insider dealing. If someone with insider knowledge breaks those rules he is likely to be punished.

Every form of game has rules and to break them is cheating, which leads to punishment. A golfer who mis-scores his card or lobs his ball out of a deep bunker instead of hitting it is likely to be expelled from his club. Cheating at golf or on the stock exchange, however, does *not* constitute corruption under my definition. There is no corruptor and there is no corruptee whose actions, for which he has responsibility, are affected by a favour received. Two highly publicised cases in the UK illustrate this.

In 2000 Piers Morgan was editor of the *Daily Mirror*. The paper's City section carried a regular feature, a share-tipping column called 'The City Slickers'. Shortly before an edition of the column appeared recommending buying shares in Viglen Technology as a hot prospect, Morgan bought shares in the company. When the *Daily Mirror*'s recommendation appeared, the value of the shares rose sharply.

The story of what Morgan had done was revealed by *Private Eye*. He was criticised by the Press Complaints Commission, which ruled that he had breached the industry's code of conduct. A DTI investigation was begun which finally reported in 2004, saying that no charges would be brought against him.

The comments of James Hipwell, one of the City Slickers team, about the DTI's conclusions were enlightening. He told the BBC's *Today* programme: 'Inevitably, some of the things we wrote about ended up being companies that we actually owned shares in … I've done nothing that a multitude of other financial hacks haven't done themselves. Share ramping, insider dealing goes on every single day.'[1]

This case may be seen by some as cheating if there are rules, for example, that require financial tipsters not to trade in the shares they tip. This apparently was not the case at the *Daily Mirror*. Indeed, a strong argument in favour of the tipsters trading in the shares they tip is: if you are that clever, put your money where your mouth is. It is clear that, under my definition, Morgan's alleged action would have been corrupt only if he had paid a consideration to the City Slickers to tip Viglen's shares so that he could make a quick killing on them. There is no evidence that he did so. His actions were not corrupt.

In an earlier example, in 1994 MAI plc made a bid for Anglia TV. Lady Mary Archer, Lord Archer's wife, was a director of Anglia and therefore had knowledge of the pending bid. There is no evidence that she passed this information to Jeffrey Archer. A flurry of activity in Anglia shares took place shortly before the bid was announced, however, and, following information from the Stock Exchange, the DTI began an investigation into those who bought shares, including Lord Archer. The media at the time

---

1   BBC News, 10 June 2004.

reported that Lord Archer had made a profit of £70,000 on his purchase of shares bought just before the bid became public.[2] Lord Archer claimed that he had bought the shares on behalf of a friend. No charges were brought against him.

If Lord Archer's claim is taken to be true his action would *not* have been corrupt under my definition. Anyone can buy shares on the stock market and therefore doing so does *not* constitute an action for which the purchaser concerned has responsibility. Insider dealing may be wrong on various levels. For example, it may be a breach of an employee's contract of employment, it may be a breach of the civil or criminal law, or it may be a breach of the rules of a stock exchange on which a company's shares have a quotation. It may be cheating and punishable under the Companies Act, but it is not corrupt.

Applying the author's definition

Throughout the rest of this book I refer to cases of public interest that have occurred within the past 25 years in many countries around the world. Having presented my definition of corruption, I suggest verdicts of 'corrupt' or 'uncorrupt' based on my five criteria. In doing this I am not making factual assertions but presenting my comments made in good faith on the facts, most of which are well known already and which are also summarised briefly in the text. Inevitably, because I am expressing an opinion in coming to these conclusions, some of the verdicts may not accord with what is the law in different jurisdictions. Thus, for example, a person may be tried on charges of fraud, perverting the

2   BBC News, 19 July 2001.

Table 1 Testing whether specific cases constitute corruption

Protagonist	Action	(1) Covert?	(2) Favour involved?	(3) Influences corruptee's action?	(4) Benefits corruptee or nominee?	(5) Within corruptee's authority?	Result: Action was corrupt?
UK							
1 A prime minister	Receives donation for his party Favours the donor's case	N	Y	Y	Y	Y	N
2 A lawyer	Obtains discounts on the purchase of flats Advises on a legal case	Y	Y	Y	Y	N	N
3 An MP	Takes cash for putting down parliamentary questions	Y	Y	Y	Y	Y	Y
Elsewhere							
4 A mayor	Gives free flats to friends/supporters	Y	Y	Y	Y	Y	Y
5 A European Commissioner	Appoints her dentist as a scientific adviser without duties	Y	Y	Y	Y	Y	Y
6 A French president	Siphons public cash into a German political party	Y	Y	Y	Y	Y	Y
7 An American president	Made his brother Attorney General	N	Y	Y	Y	Y	Y
8 A middle-east despot	Gave sons key government posts	N	Y	Y	Y	Y	N
9 A middle-east despot	Built palaces with oil revenues	N	N	N	Y	Y	N
10 Wall Street analyst	Gave clients intentionally flawed advice to benefit his firm	Y	Y	Y	Y	Y	Y
Generalist examples							
11 Traffic policeman	Demands cash so as not to issue a ticket	Y	Y	Y	Y	Y	Y
12 Government official	Requires percentage of contract value	Y	Y	Y	Y	Y	Y
13 Purchasing officer	Chooses a supplier, receives crate of whisky	Y	Y	Y	Y	Y	Y
14 Roman tax collector	Kept some of the tax he collected	N	N	Y	Y	Y	N

Source: Ian Senior, 2006

course of justice or simply lying in court without the word 'corruption' appearing in the charge sheet. They may be found guilty or not guilty of these other charges. Thus the opinions set out in my verdicts in relation to corruption do not necessarily coincide with the findings of fact or law of the jurisdiction concerned or with the courts' verdicts. As stated earlier, this, I believe, is the strength of my definition, in enabling me to make comparisons across different countries, institutions, actions and circumstances. Some of my verdicts may seem surprising.

I believe that the purpose of economics is to apply economic theory to real life in politics, government, management and society, so let us test whether my definition proves helpful in some specific cases. In the following table, using my definition with its five criteria, each case is found to entail corruption or not to do so. Of the fourteen following cases six do not constitute corruption though in loose parlance they might be described as such. The variety of the examples in the table suggests that my definition is a useful tool. I now give explanations about why the action concerned is classified as corrupt or uncorrupt.

CASE 1

A political party receives a donation. The prime minister appears to favour the donor's case in new draft legislation relating to tobacco advertising.

Verdict: a near-miss but uncorrupt. Notes of the meeting between Tony Blair and Bernie Ecclestone were recorded by a civil servant and later made publicly available

COMMENT

In May 1997 the Labour Party returned to power after an election dominated by cases of 'sleaze' that had dogged John Major's outgoing Conservative administration. Towards the end of 1997, however, Tony Blair himself became embroiled in an affair involving a donation of £1 million to the Labour Party by Bernie Ecclestone, the owner of Formula One racing. More details of this affair are given later. What saves Tony Blair from being judged corrupt under my definition is that the meeting between himself and Mr Ecclestone was recorded by his private secretary, a senior civil servant, and notes of the meeting were released to the press when the media were in pursuit of details. Mr Ecclestone's donation was returned by the Labour Party, an admission that the Labour Party was wrong to accept it as a key to opening the door of Number 10 Downing Street.

This affair was the first of various incidents that have tarnished Labour's commitment to be beyond reproach in such matters, and it helped to give rise to a new act passed by the Labour government, the Political Parties Elections and Referendums Act 2002 (PPERA). Under this Act donations of over £1,000 to individuals and over £5,000 to parties must be reported to the Electoral Commission, which then makes them public.

The Ecclestone affair highlights the importance of *covertness* as a condition in defining cases of corruption. In the USA, for example, it is commonplace for wealthy donors of campaign funds to expect a payback in the form of a political appointment, the enactment of specific legislation or the inclusion of a state-funded activity within a programme of interest to the donor. The practice is widely accepted and is known as 'pork barrel'. It particularly affects members of the House of Representatives, who, notably in the second year of their two-year term, make strenuous efforts to have particular projects in their districts funded by the federal government. This is done by tacking projects on to a much larger financial Bill going through Congress.

Does 'pork barrel' represent corruption? No, because the allocation of the funds is overt. All members of the House of Representatives are free to read and vote against 'pork barrel' items in the Bill concerned. Few oppose other members' 'pork barrel' because they want their own bit of pork to be granted too.

CASE 2

A high-profile lawyer obtains a discount on the purchase of flats and then advises on a legal case for the person who procured the discount.

Verdict: uncorrupt

COMMENT

This case centred on Cherie Blair, the prime minister's wife, concerning transactions that were intended to be covert. An apparent exchange of the value of the discount on flats for legal advice by Cherie Blair consisted, however, of barter, which is not corrupt. There is no suggestion that Cherie Blair had any authority of her own or through Tony Blair to influence judicial proceedings that were pending against Peter Foster, the procurer of the discount. Initially she denied her involvement with Peter Foster until e-mails she had sent him were published. Despite her later public apology, this was in my view reprehensible from a person in her position who acts as a judge as well as a QC, but it does not constitute corruption.

In a case with interesting parallels Hutchcroft (1997) gives a telling quotation from the *New York Times*.

'I am me,' explains Singaporean Senior Minister Lee Kuan Yew in response to criticism that he derived substantial personal advantage from a recent deal involving luxury condominiums. 'It's not a level playing field'. The benefit to Lee Kuan Yew and his son, Deputy Prime Minister Lee Hsien Loong, consisted of discounts of more than $700,000 [£385,000] in a 'soft sale' of condominiums conducted before bids were opened to the public.

This case is particularly noteworthy because Singapore was and still is considered to be remarkably uncorrupt by world standards, and notably by comparison with neighbouring states such as Indonesia, the Philippines and Thailand, in all of which corruption is prevalent. Indeed, Singapore's reputation for uncorruption combined with a liberal, market-based economy has been a major factor in the huge influx of foreign investment that helped bring its GDP per head in 2001, adjusted by purchasing power, to US$22,456 compared with US$25,141 in the UK.

Within the world of property the opportunity for the vendor of the Singaporean condominiums to tell prospective purchasers that some had been bought by the two Lees would have had tangible commercial value, justifying the discount. The endorsement of products and services by sporting and other celebrities is an accepted part of marketing for which substantial fees are paid. David Beckham is reputed to earn £15 million per year from endorsements compared with a modest £5 million from playing football for Real Madrid.

The sale of condominiums to the Lees was made before bids became open to the general public, but given that the vendor was a private company, the discount reflected a legitimate transaction. At auctions lots can be sold by private treaty before the auction, if the vendor agrees. The Lees' action would have been corrupt only if the discount given by the vendor required reciprocal covert action(s) on the part of the Lees which fell within their authority as the republic's two leading politicians. This has not been suggested.

CASE 3

An MP takes cash for putting down parliamentary questions.

Verdict: corrupt

COMMENT

A case that occurred in the mid-1990s in the UK caused a major political scandal. Mohamed Al Fayed, the owner of Harrods, declared that he had paid cash in brown envelopes to two MPs to gain their influence. Specifically he claimed that they tabled parliamentary questions on his behalf. One MP, Tim Smith, admitted his guilt and left the House of Commons. The other, Neil Hamilton, to this day denies the charge and has taken court action to try to prove his innocence. He lost his seat in the 1997 general election and has not returned to politics.

Consider only the MP who admitted his guilt. The case is clearly one of corruption even though the influence of individual backbenchers' questions on the government of the day is small. The case transgressed, however, the fundamental British code of politics at national and local level under which politicians who have a personal, financial or other interest in a matter under their authority declare it publicly and take no part in its discussion or decisions relating to it. In local government, as *Private Eye* has chronicled over the years in its column 'Rotten Boroughs', scandals have regularly occurred in which the chairs of local planning committees have used their positions to give planning permission to property developers, taking bribes or other favours in return.

The sleaze cases of the 1990s have given rise to registers of interests that apply not just to parliamentarians but to members of numerous government bodies as well.

CASE 4

A French mayor allocates rent-free flats to friends and supporters.

Verdict: corrupt if proven

COMMENT

In France political corruption, described later, is endemic. One of the accusations against President Chirac is that, when he was mayor of Paris in the 1990s, kickbacks were required from building and other contractors that were paid to his party or to individuals. A further charge is that he awarded flats owned by the city of Paris to friends and party officials rent-free or at peppercorn rents. As president of the French Republic Mr Chirac is immune from prosecution, but when his term of office expires in 2007 he may face criminal proceedings, so no charges have been proved as yet.

If Mr Chirac's actions are shown to be as stated, the *covert* award of high-quality public accommodation at below-market rents to 'cronies' to ensure or reward their loyalty is clearly corrupt under my definition. This may point to a cultural difference in France as regards the funding of politics. In France it seems that when political parties accept payments from contractors who have received public contracts, this is not perceived as corruption and only becomes corrupt if some of the money remains with individual politicians. Under my definition the favours concerned benefit the *nominees* of the politicians concerned, and so constitute corruption. It is clear that the money, in whoever's pockets it finally lies, benefits the political careers of the politicians who become elected.

In the UK there are resonances with criticism that was voiced in the House of Commons in 2002. A cross-party committee of MPs investigated the rents charged to minor members of the royal family who were living in luxurious flats in Kensington Palace, which is owned by the state. In some cases the rents were less than £100 per week at an estimated cost to the taxpayer of around £15 million each year in terms of cash forgone by the exchequer.[3]

This practice may be described as discreditable since minor royals undertake few public duties, but it is not corrupt. First, the rents are in the public domain, although they were not always so. Second, it is not obvious what *favours* the minor royals have given to the Queen or to others to influence their *actions* in the matter. It would be difficult to show that in this matter the Queen was either a corruptor or a corruptee. Patronage of this sort may be objectionable but it does not conform to my five criteria and it is therefore not corrupt.

A further example in the same vein is the valuable accommodation bestowed free by Tony Blair, the prime minister, on

3   www.themovechannel.com/ssitefeatures/news/2002-june/4b.asp.

Margaret Beckett, then his environment secretary, and on David Blunkett, then a backbench MP, following his resignation as home secretary and later as work and pensions secretary. Neither was entitled to official accommodation or to official protection. Despite her free accommodation Margaret Beckett is reported to have claimed £50,000 tax-free expenses for a house in her Derbyshire constituency which she owns outright.[4] David Blunkett, who resigned over a scandal relating to fast-tracking a residence permit for his mistress's nanny, still has no entitlement to state accommodation.[5] However objectionable Mr Blair's largesse may be, these favours at taxpayers' expense are overt. Mr Chirac's alleged favours, on the other hand, were covert.

CASE 5

A European Commissioner appoints her dentist as a scientific adviser to the Commission with a salary but no duties for which he was qualified.

Verdict: corrupt if proven

COMMENT

In 1999 a whistle-blower in the European Commission, Paul van Buitenen, produced a dossier of cases that alleged corruption in the EC. These included evidence that Edith Cresson, the French commissioner for education and research and a former French prime minister, had awarded research contracts to her dentist, René Berthelot. Jacques Santer, then the Commission's president,

---

4   *The Times*, 11 April 2005, p. 6.

5   Ibid.

and all the other commissioners resigned, evidently to show solidarity with Mrs Cresson. Five years later, in June 2004, the EC's court of first instance ruled there were no grounds for prosecution of Mrs Cresson or any of her co-defendants. There was no denial that Mrs Cresson had signed employment documents in Mr Berthelot's favour worth a total of around €150,000 (£100,000). Nor has it been said that Mr Berthelot was qualified to be a scientific adviser in the subject area concerned. Nor has it been argued that the few pages of notes he sent to the Commission by way of fulfilment of his contract(s) were relevant or useful. The court reached its decision to drop charges against Mrs Cresson during a closed-door hearing.[6]

The delay and the outcome of the case are disturbing. The employment documents for Mr Berthelot were a factual matter that could have been resolved in five days rather than five years. If the dentist was carrying out research other than on Edith Cresson's teeth, this could have been established in a further five days. Slowing down the legal process is a classic method used by politicians wishing to take the heat out of awkward situations. A hearing behind closed doors was unjustifiable in dealing with simple matters of fact and suggests that the court did not wish dirty linen to be washed in public.

Mrs Cresson's action of adding her dentist to the EC's payroll is undisputed. The financial *favours* he received are known. The awarding of the contracts was *covert*. Did they influence *actions* over which he had *authority*? If he gave her free dentistry in return, the answer becomes 'yes', though as he is now dead we may never know what occurred. If these acts took place as alleged, I would

6   www.eubusiness.com, 30 June 2004.

classify the awarding of these contracts as corrupt, though they also have the flavour of nepotism or stealing, which, as I explain elsewhere, fall outside my definition of corruption.

CASE 6

A president siphons cash into a political party.

Verdict: corrupt

COMMENT

In France and Italy a standard practice in the 1980s and 1990s was for public works contractors to be required to pay a percentage of the value of public works to the political party of the authority that awarded the contracts. Various arguments have been made to justify this practice, but it is corrupt.

The first argument used is that political parties are essential to democracy and that fund-raising is difficult if the state does not provide funds. The second is the concept mentioned earlier and apparently widely accepted in France, that if the kickbacks do not go to specific individuals for their personal use, then kickbacks do not amount to corruption.

Both justifications are flawed. The power of money to influence elections is known and demonstrated, not least in the USA, where war chests of many millions are needed to hire party workers and to buy prime-time television. Thus, money paid to political parties benefits the candidates of those parties. They in turn get elected and benefit directly from the public purse in terms of salaries, accommodation and allowances. In addition, in the French and Italian cases the politicians gained the power to choose more public contractors and so to coerce them into paying further contributions to their political party. Thus the cycle in France and Italy was not only corrupt but was self-reinforcing.

The question of 'cash for honours' is current in the UK. The issue at the time of writing is whether gifts or loans by donors to political parties, particularly to the party in power, influence the award of honours and the appointment of life peers.

In this case the key test is whether the donations were *covert* or *overt*. Under the PPERA law introduced by the Labour government in 2000 and mentioned earlier, all donations above £5,000 to political parties must be reported to the Electoral Commission, which then publishes them. Thus significant donations now become *overt* and, even if they result in the award of honours and peerages, cannot be described as corrupt.

The emergence of the fact that a considerable number of wealthy individuals have made undeclared *loans* to the Labour and Conservative parties exploits a loophole in the law which needs to be closed. A loan made by a bank cannot be regarded as a *favour*, so a loan by an individual or a firm made on strictly the same terms as a bank's also cannot be termed a favour. On the other hand, if the loan from an individual or firm is more favourable than that of a commercial bank in terms of the rate of interest, the terms of repayment or the collateral required, then the value of these differences clearly constitutes a favour. To avoid such uncertainties, it would be best if all *loans* to political parties above £5,000 also had to be declared to and reported by the Electoral Commission.

To ensure full transparency it would be desirable that when peers are appointed or other honours awarded to those who have provided declarable donations or loans to political parties, these details are included in their citations in the honours lists. This would enable voters to know in particular to what extent the House of Lords, which still has some modest legislative power, is influenced by political appointees who have given significantly to the political parties and so benefited the politicians who nominated them for appointment.

CASES 7 AND 8

An American president makes his brother Attorney General and an Iraqi president puts his sons in charge of the army and the secret police.

Verdict: uncorrupt

COMMENT

One of President Kennedy's first appointments was that of his brother, Robert, to be Attorney General. Decades later Saddam Hussein appointed his sons Uday and Qusay to positions of power in his tyrannical administration. Under my definition none of these appointments was corrupt because they were all overt.

This may surprise readers who think nepotism or cronyism to be a form of corruption. Logic, however, does not support this view. The appointment of subordinates always takes account of the appointee's ability to satisfy the appointer's requirements. Loyalty, trust and the ability to work together are important in harmonious and fruitful working, particularly in political relationships, given that politicians, by the nature of their calling and ambitions, are prone to disloyalty.

Nepotism in business is not considered corrupt when Jones

& Sons are on the letterhead. The correct counterbalance to nepotism in public life is that the legislature should have the power to veto the appointment of unsuitable senior staff by the executive. The US Congress investigates and sometimes vetoes the President's nominees for the most senior jobs. Although this may reflect political motivation, the process has the merit of putting a spotlight on candidates' backgrounds, their strengths and weaknesses and their overall suitability for the post concerned. Supreme Court nominees have recently been rejected in this way. Of course, if the president had covertly offered members of the relevant committee of Congress favours to give his nominee a soft ride in the investigation's hearings, that would indeed have been corrupt.

In essence, the potential for nepotism in executive positions needs to be counterbalanced by democratic powers to block unsuitable appointments. Overt nepotism reflects weak democratic systems rather than corruption.

CASE 9

A despot builds palaces with wealth acquired in office.

Verdict: probably uncorrupt

COMMENT

Numerous presidents, generally of impoverished countries, have acquired vast wealth and spent it on lavish abodes: for example, Emperor Bokassa of the Central African Republic, President Mobutu of the Congo, President Ceausescu of Romania, President Mugabe of Zimbabwe and, spectacularly, President Saddam

Hussein of Iraq. It would be tempting to describe these residences as the fruits of corruption on a massive scale.

In some cases, no doubt, there has indeed been massive corruption. For example, if a despot takes a percentage of the value of contracts awarded for oil concessions, does so covertly and influences the choice of contractors, this is corruption. In the case of the absolute despots mentioned above, however, covert bribes may have been unnecessary. The presidents concerned simply used public funds as their own. Such presidents *steal* from the national treasury. As noted earlier, it is important to separate corruption from stealing. In essence, a sumptuous palace may reflect kleptocracy resulting from failed judicial, legal and democratic systems rather than from corruption as I define it.

CASE 10

A Wall Street analyst gives flawed advice to clients in order to benefit his firm.

Verdict: corrupt

COMMENT

Financial analysts and racing tipsters believe that analysis of data provides better returns to their clients than sticking a pin into a list of companies to invest in or horses to back. Financial analysts are well paid, but this has not prevented some in the USA from publishing flawed advice about the value of shares in companies that also placed business with the analysts' own companies.

These examples of corruption lie entirely within the private sector. Giving wantonly bad advice was corrupt because the managements were rewarding the analysts with wantonly high salaries. In doing so they were increasing their companies' revenue as a result of the bad advice that they knowingly published.

CASE 11

A traffic policeman demands cash so as not to issue a speeding ticket.

Verdict: corrupt

COMMENT

In many developing countries policemen and minor officials are extremely easy to bribe, not least when they are badly paid by local standards. In the countries of the former Soviet Union, even before the collapse of communism, corruption was rife. In 1988 over 100,000 police officers were sacked: 15 per cent of the entire Soviet police force. Since the collapse of communism little has changed. In 1993 Boris Yeltsin stated publicly that 'Corruption is devouring the state from top to bottom' (Sterling, 1994).

Those who argue that corruption is the oil that makes state machinery run better might say that giving a small sum to a policeman to avoid a speeding ticket is an efficient transaction if the sum is less than the cost of issuing and collecting a fine. This argument is false. Police become better off by demanding bribes rather than by enforcing the law. If serious criminals realise that the police are corrupt they are able to pay larger bribes to escape court cases and prison. Police corruption then becomes endemic.

CASES 12 AND 13

An official requires a percentage of the value of a contract.

Verdict: corrupt if covert

COMMENT

If an official requires a percentage of a contract's value, this normally fulfils the five criteria of my definition of corruption. There can, however, be circumstances that would change the verdict. In tenders for Saudi Arabian contracts some years ago it was required in the tendering specifications that a local agent be engaged who would receive a specified percentage such as 10–15 per cent of the contract's value. Usually the agents provided no input to the work but simply added their names to the bid. British firms and those of other nations did not consider this to be corruption because the Saudi ministries overtly instructed bidders that an agent should be appointed on these terms.

In the West it was believed that this system enabled the Saudi authorities to capture and distribute to local people some of the value of its oil wealth. In practice it added a premium to bids because if the firm's most economical bid would have been 100, a 15 per cent payment to the agent meant that the bid became 115. In France and other countries for many years the legitimacy of bribing foreign officials to gain business was recognised by the tax authorities as a legitimate expense to charge against tax.

CASE 14

A tax collector of the Roman empire keeps some of the tax he collects.

Verdict: uncorrupt

COMMENT

In Roman days and at other times the collection of taxes was a rudimentary business. Given the near-absence of communications and of accounting systems in Roman days, the requirement that a tax collector should collect an open-ended amount of tax and pass a pre-determined amount up the line to higher authority was accepted as a practical way of doing things. It was overt. Corruption became an issue only if would-be tax collectors paid covert bribes to the higher authorities to have themselves appointed as tax collectors or if individual taxpayers were able to bribe tax collectors to avoid paying tax.

Summary

From the discussion of the foregoing cases it can be seen that applying my definition generally produces clear results in determining whether a given action constitutes corruption or not. Theft is not corruption. Fraud is not corruption. Nepotism, though potentially undemocratic, is not corruption. Insider dealing is not corruption. Cheating is not corruption. Selling peerages overtly is not corruption. All these things may nevertheless be objectionable and weaken the fabric of society. These examples and the explanations I have given lay down a basis for the remainder of this book. They have the merit of exemplifying in practical terms what constitutes corruption and what does not.

2   CASES OF CORRUPTION: AWARDING MEDALS

Corruption is extremely difficult to measure because by defini-tion it is covert. When individual cases of corruption come to light it is sometimes possible to put a monetary value on them because the value of the bribe or other favour becomes known. In general it might seem plausible that the bigger the bribe the more heinous the corruption, but this is uncertain.

Consider two examples:

a) A civil engineering firm winning a foreign contract worth £100 million covertly pays £2 million to the functionary who awarded the contract.
b) A minister covertly receives £1 million from an industrial pressure group to modify legislation under his authority.

Case (a) might seem twice as corrupt as Case (b), yet many have argued that Case (a) represents a form of necessary marketing expenditure in certain countries. If the rates of bribery are known and all bidders for the contract offer broadly the same level of bribe, then not to offer a bribe is self-defeating. If all bidders offer identical bribes, the competitive playing field becomes level because the corruptee has no additional benefit from a particular bribe and should therefore choose the contractor on technical merit.

By contrast Case (b) seems much more reprehensible. Social justice, the legal system and ultimately the quality of life all depend on laws being passed and implemented that represent the working of a democratic system in which the election of legislators and their actions broadly reflect the wishes of the majority. If the bribing of law-makers by special interests is permitted to distort the laws that are passed, the quality of life of the majority suffers because their wishes are bypassed.

From Examples (a) and (b) I conclude that the value and extent of corruption cannot easily be related to the value of favours in individual cases that come to light. I therefore put forward another method that does not rely on the value of the favours but rather on the rank of the corruptors and corruptees.

In the following cases of corruption in selected international bodies and countries I focus on four tiers of people and, in the manner of athletic competitions, I award medals for what, using my definition, constitutes either proven or prima facie corruption. Again, these are subjective comments. I have based the expression of my honestly held beliefs on facts that are already substantially matters of public debate, and I have also summarised the background details.

Prima facie corruption, as opposed to proven corruption, may occur, for example, where an individual has received a payment covertly (when the normal rules do not allow the acceptance of such payments without declaration), when the individual has the authority to influence an action that would benefit the corruptor, but where there is no clear evidence that the action or benefit has been delivered to the corruptor. I accept that laws and customs in some jurisdictions might not judge the individuals to be corrupt. It is very important to note that the underlying purpose of this chapter is not to describe the actions of particular individuals or to make factual allegations about their guilt or innocence but to uncover situations where particular legal regimes are inadequate and/or where particular corrupt or potentially corrupt actions have taken place. In the case of prima facie corruption it should be clear that the laws of a particular country might not prohibit payments to people who have authority to deliver a favour and also that the favour hoped for when payments are made to those in authority may never be delivered. Nevertheless, if the legal system allows such covert payments it is, in my view, a system that implicitly encourages corruption, and that should be highlighted.

It is also important to note that medals are awarded to countries and not to people. As also becomes clear later in the book, the absence of proper legal procedures to deal with corruption is, in itself, a serious matter and encourages systemic corruption. Therefore I award medals to countries either where corruption is proven, guilt admitted or resignations have taken place or where I believe that the legal system has not allowed guilt or innocence to be proven in public. In some cases this is because investigations take place behind closed doors (for example, in the EC) and in other cases because particular politicians have legal immunities.

Medals are awarded on the following basis:

a) gold medals: presidents and prime ministers
b) silver medals: ministers and senior functionaries such as heads of state agencies;
c) bronze medals: law-makers such as members of parliament, judges, high-level corporate executives and high-level policemen;
d) nickel medals: middle-to-low-ranking functionaries,

middle-to-low-ranking corporate executives, ordinary-level policemen and miscellaneous employees in the private sector such as football referees.

The concept of awarding medals for corruption in this way has not appeared previously in economic literature or elsewhere. Some will say that the availability of information varies between countries. This is true. In states with restrictive regulations imposed by government it may be difficult or impossible to publish stories about corruption. In other states corruption is so endemic as not to be newsworthy.

A further point is that the amount of money that needs to be involved in a corruption scandal for it to become noteworthy varies from country to country. In the UK, Jonathan Aitken, a Conservative minister, accepted free nights in a Paris hotel worth perhaps £2,000 as a favour and ultimately resigned from office. In other countries kickbacks to ministers or prime ministers need to be in the millions before they become noticed.

The merit of the medal system is that it sets out to describe the tip of the iceberg that becomes visible in individual jurisdictions and institutions. With real icebergs, the part above water enables the mass below water to be calculated accurately. In my system there is as yet no means of estimating the corruption that lies below the surface from the corruption that is visible above the surface. It seems probable, however, that when a president or prime minister is transparently corrupt, as in much of Africa, corruption extends down to the roots of society. Identifying and describing the tip of an iceberg is a useful start in that it identifies the problem occurring below the waterline which requires further investigation.

Strict academics may frown on my system for the reasons I have given. By contrast, ordinary people may find the system and the medals table enlightening.

The time frame I have chosen is the period 1980 to the present. Corrupt events during the past 25 years should provide insight into which international institutions and countries tolerate or suffer from corruption.

The information gathered on corruption cases is drawn from books, newspapers and the Internet. My search has been extensive but does not claim to be comprehensive. For this reason the medals table that concludes this chapter is indicative rather than definitive.

The medals table covers EU-15 but not the ten accession states that joined the EU in 2004 to make it EU-25, or the four current candidate states: Bulgaria, Croatia, Romania and Turkey. I provide information about accession and candidate states but I have not tried to award medals because in some cases their levels of corruption are so high that the medals system is inappropriate. I have included information on some of the world's main non-EU industrialised countries: Australia, Canada, Japan, Russia, Switzerland and the USA. Russia is described but has been excluded from the medals table, again because its level of corruption is so high.

Further, I exclude from the medals table the whole of Africa, Asia, the Middle East and Latin America. In many countries within these regions kleptocracy renders corruption unnecessary, while in many others corruption is endemic.

In awarding the medals I have made appropriate use of publicly available information. There is a sense in which all medals are provisional in that new information can come to light – either to undermine a prima facie case of corruption or to strengthen the evidence. As noted above, corrupt activity is not necessarily criminal, and I have awarded medals for activities that fit my economic definition of corruption given above. Those who would use a different definition might award medals differently.

Corruption in international agencies

In this and the following chapters I give brief details of corruption cases in the organisations and states concerned. Where available I give monetary values of the sums involved. Currency conversions into pounds sterling are indicative only because of changing exchange rates over time and the fact that many of the corruption scandals took place over a period of years.

United Nations secretariat

From 2000 to 2003 the UN went through the tortuous process of drafting a convention against corruption. Corruption was described as a trillion-dollar scourge, though how this figure was estimated is unclear. In Merida, Mexico, in December 2003, 94 countries signed the convention. The convention requires countries to criminalise a range of corrupt activities, to take action to promote integrity and prevent corruption, and to cooperate with other states in combating corruption. For example, it establishes legal mechanisms for the return of looted assets that have been transferred to other states.

On paper, therefore, the UN as an institution is against corruption, so the example its secretariat sets in the workings of its own organisation should be transparent and exemplary. Recently, Iraq's oil-for-food programme has raised grave doubts about some of the UN's functionaries. Paul Volcker's report in August 2005 showed that the programme was at least in part a vehicle for corruption. The report estimated that kickbacks to a value of US$1.8 billion were paid in connection with the contracts of 2,392 companies.[1] The committee found that before Saddam Hussein's overthrow Benon Sevan, the UN official in charge of the programme, steered oil contracts to African Middle East Petroleum, a company belonging to a friend, which earned $1.5 million (£800,000) by reselling more than 7 million barrels of Iraqi crude oil between 1998 and 2001.

Volcker's interim report said Sevan's solicitations of Iraqi officials on behalf of his friend's company were a 'grave and continuing conflict of interest ... ethically improper and seriously undermined the integrity of the United Nations', and that the Iraqi government had hoped Sevan would act favourably in return for the allocations. Volcker's final report accused Benon Sevan of receiving at least $160,000 (£86,000) in kickbacks.[2] When asked to explain receiving four cash payments between 1999 and 2003 Sevan is reported as saying these came from his Cypriot aunt. Her retirement income before she died in 2004 was £460 a month.[3] Just before the publication of the Volcker report, Sevan resigned and flew to Cyprus, from where he cannot be extradited should the USA's courts wish to press charges against him.

Verdict: A silver medal for Sevan.

---

1   Independent Inquiry Committee into the United Nations Oil-for-Food Programme, *Report on Programme Manipulation*, 27 October 2005, p. 1.
2   *The Times*, 9 August 2005, p. 25.
3   Ibid., 5 February 2005, p. 40.

European Commission

The European Commission is the source of all EU legislation, notably directives and regulations. These can be amended or rejected by the European Parliament, but the latter cannot initiate legislation. Further, the Commission is the first point of adjudication over its own legislation. References to the European Court of First Instance and the European Court of Justice are possible, but these take years to produce judgments. Given the snail's pace of these two courts, the EC's functionaries enjoy huge legislative, executive and judicial powers.

Within my chosen time frame there has been one major corruption scandal concerning a commissioner, Mrs Edith Cresson, and innumerable and continuing lesser fraud and corruption scandals.

Edith Cresson

The case of Mrs Edith Cresson, a former French prime minister and European commissioner, has been discussed earlier. Although the charges by the Belgian authorities concerning fraud and abuse have been dropped, there is no dispute about her role in hiring her dentist, the late René Berthelot, as an EU adviser on HIV/Aids, a subject about which he had no competence. He received some £100,000 for two years' work, during which he produced a total of 24 pages of notes subsequently deemed to be of no value.[4]

Verdict: Mrs Cresson is a former prime minister of France, but the contracts she gave her dentist occurred when she was

---

4   Andrew Osborn, *Guardian*, 26 March 2003.

a European commissioner. A silver medal is awarded because the European Commission's investigation of this case was not undertaken in an open and transparent way.

Eurostat
In September 2003 the EC Commission took notice of allegations by one of its staff, Dorte Schmidt-Brown, that during the 1990s officials of Eurostat, the Commission's statistical service, channelled hundred of thousands of euros into unofficial bank accounts and that former colleagues and family members set up companies that then received contracts from Eurostat. Concerns had been sounded years before by internal auditors, but it was only in May 2003 that three Eurostat officials were suspended from duty. Eurostat is thought to have siphoned off almost €5 million (£3 million), most of which went missing between 1996 and 2001. The officials concerned claimed that they set up the private bank accounts so that they could pay contractors more quickly.

The Commission's record under the then commissioner Neil Kinnock in supporting whistle-blowers is poor, and Dorte Schmidt-Brown remains suspended on sick leave.

Verdict: Three bronze medals for the principal Eurostat staff concerned.

Whistle-blowing in the European Commission[5]
When Neil Kinnock became a commissioner in 1999 with respons-

---

5   Various newspaper reports.

ibility for cleaning up the Commission, he promised zero tolerance. Little appears to have changed on his watch.

In the early 2000s, Robert McCoy, a British official working for the Committee of the Regions (CoR), discovered systematic cheating on expense claims by members attending meetings of the committee. Next he discovered apparent fraud in relation to two printing contracts placed with an outside company. He asked for the Commission's specialist fraud unit to be informed and was rebuffed by his secretary-general, Mr Vincenzo Falcone. Shortly afterwards he discovered that a further contract, worth up to €270,000 (£189,000) over three years, had been promised to the same company without proper competing tenders. Senior managers put pressure on him to allow the contract to go ahead, but he refused and stalled for more than six months. Since then his life has been made a misery. Shunned by colleagues, shouted at and even spat at, he is aware that everyone wants to get rid of him and is looking for grounds to do so.[6]

In 1999 an EC official, Paul van Buitenen, went public with details of corruption, cronyism and abuse of power in the Commission. Three years later he said that he could see no change in Brussels and decided to return to the Netherlands because the pressure in Brussels became too much to bear.

In 2002 Marta Andreasen was sacked as the EU's chief accountant after saying publicly that the EU accounting system was riddled with mistakes and loopholes. Again Vice-President Neil Kinnock had to defend himself against suggestions that he was trying to gag a whistle-blower who had accused him of ignoring her warnings of deficiencies in the EU accounting system.

6   www.telegraph.co.uk/news/main.jhtml?xml=/news/2003/09/28/whistle128.
    xml.

He told the European Parliament's budgetary control committee that 'We are doing our damnedest to ensure there are accounting changes to address complaints about wrongdoing. Any evidence from staff is seriously treated, and there is career security for genuine whistle-blowers. She had not followed correct procedures, and her behaviour would not have been tolerated by any civil service in the democratic world.'

Despite these words there seems to be little appetite within the Commission for cleaning up fake expenses claims, fraudulent contracts and phoney payments. The internal auditors have refused to sign off the Commission's accounts for eleven successive years, and whistle-blowers are sidelined and persecuted.

Verdict: In my view, Mr Vincenzo Falcone should have fully investigated Mr McCoy's claims of fraud and corruption, but unless it can be shown that he covertly benefited from not taking action, he cannot be awarded a medal.

OLAF

The European Commission's anti-fraud office is known as OLAF. Its task is: 'to fight fraud and corruption in complete independence. An anti-fraud organisation does not require or seek popularity. Rather, it needs to earn respect through the quality of its work, through its results, and by demonstrating integrity and an ability to take the right decisions under pressure'.[7]

How well is OLAF achieving its mission, particularly in relation to corruption? At first sight there appears to be cause for

---

7   Introduction to OLAF's annual report, 2003/04.

Table 2 **OLAF: cases by type, 30 June 2004**

	Internal investigation	External investigation	Co-ordinated cases	Assisting cases	Total
Agriculture	0	24	53	12	89
Alcohol	0	0	1	0	1
Anti-corruption	44	0	0	4	48
Cigarettes	0	3	37	8	48
Customs	0	43	41	0	84
Direct expenditure	1	36	0	10	47
Eurostat	8	2	0	0	10
External aid	0	62	1	14	77
Multi-agency investigations	0	5	0	1	6
Precursors	0	0	11	0	11
Structural funds	0	39	7	13	59
Trade	0	2	2	1	5
VAT	0	0	18	8	26
Grand total	53	216	171	71	511

Source: OLAF annual report, 2003/04, p. 28,www.europa.eu.int/olaf

guarded optimism. Of 53 cases being investigated internally by OLAF in June 2005, 44 relate to corruption. Eurostat is separated out to account for a further eight cases. Together with one other case relating to direct expenditure, these 53 cases represent 10 per cent of the total of 511 cases under investigation. In other words, OLAF has plenty of work on hand.

OLAF analyses in detail how many cases it is dealing with or has dealt with. It states that the total estimated financial impact for all cases in follow-up at the end of the reporting period amounted to more than €1.5 billion (£1 billion), and it says that 443 cases were closed during the reporting period, of which 209 required further follow-up.[8] There is, however, a fundamental omission. In 83 pages, despite a large number of analytical tables

8   Ibid., p. 7.

and some anonymous case studies, there are no data for successful outcomes in terms of convictions.

Follow-up may entail asking the courts, both national and European, to take action, but what about corrupt individuals within the Commission's own services? Some have been found guilty, OLAF admits, but how many? Have they been removed from office? Have they been fined or imprisoned? After five years of operation OLAF should be able to provide this key information along with the welter of other statistics that are of much less interest.

The sources of information for OLAF's work are given in the report. 'Informants' account for 34 per cent and 'Freephone' for five per cent. Thus 39 per cent of the information comes from individuals rather than institutions. In the light of the treatment of whistle-blowers described above, this is surprising and welcome.

Verdict: A considerable number of medals should be awarded to the EC but OLAF's report is too opaque to award medals accurately. A token 25 bronze medals are awarded.

Corruption in EU-15

The most valuable tool available that compares corruption between countries is Transparency International's Corruption Perceptions Index ('CPI'), which has been published annually over the past decade. In 2004 it measured and ranked 146 countries. More details are given later. In the following reports on individual states, their ranking in the CPI 2004 is quoted. Number one, Finland, is the highest-ranking country for uncorruption and Bangladesh and Haiti represent the two most corrupt countries, ranked =146.

Austria: CPI rank 15

The Austrian penal code contains penalties for bribery that include a fine of up to €500 (£350) per day for up to 360 days (€175,000/£126,000), or up to two years' imprisonment for the payer of a bribe and up to five years' imprisonment for the recipient of a bribe. Any person who bribes a civil servant, a foreign official or a manager of an Austrian public enterprise is subject to these criminal penalties.[9]

An Internet search found no reported cases of economic corruption.

Verdict: No medals.

Belgium: CPI rank =17

A characteristic of the Belgian economy is its very large informal market. Van Hove (1997) found that in 1991 only 40 per cent of the stock of currency was used for legal transactions. Another 30 per cent was likely to be hoarded, and the remaining 30 per cent was likely to be in use in the underground economy. Informal markets are not themselves corrupt within my definition but, as shown later, a high incidence of informal markets is associated with corruption.

Willy Claes and the Agusta affair

Willy Claes was Belgium's deputy prime minister on five occasions and was economics minister some years earlier. While holding

---

9   US Department of State briefing, www.state.gov/e/eb/ifd/2005/41952.htm.

that office, in 1988 he signed a contract for helicopters with the Italian firm Agusta. The Agusta affair, as it became known, arose out of an investigation into the murder of a senior member of the Socialist Party, André Cools, who was shot dead in 1991 after hinting that he would expose his party's corrupt activities. Willy Claes later became NATO's secretary-general. In December 1998 he was found guilty of accepting bribes from Agusta that were paid to the Socialist Party. The former defence minister, Guy Coeme, was given a two-year suspended sentence. The former prime minister, Guy Spitaels, and Serge Dassault, head of France's Dassault aviation concern, were convicted of corruption.

Verdict: A gold medal for Mr Spitaels as a prime minister. Mr Claes and Mr Coeme earn silver medals as ministers. A nickel medal for Mr Dassault is carried across to France's medals.

Denmark: CPI rank =3

An Internet search found no references to corruption in Denmark.

Verdict: No medals.

Finland: CPI rank 1

Only a few people are convicted of bribery each year in Finland. According to official statistics Finland prosecuted 25 bribery cases between 1985 and 1992.[10]

---

10 Department for Communication and Culture/Unit for Promotion and Publications, Helsinki.

In 2002, according to a Finnish broadcasting service, four senior employees at the Finnish National Maritime Directorate, including the director general, were charged with having taken bribes in connection with the hiring of ice-breakers to a Norwegian company.[11]

Verdict: If the parties concerned were proven guilty, medals would be awarded.

France: CPI rank =22 with Spain

In the 1980s and 1990s corruption grew to epidemic proportions in France. National and local politicians were heavily implicated, including President Chirac, then mayor of Paris. Currently he has presidential immunity from prosecution, but his colleagues during the period do not. In March 2005 47 politicians and other officials were on trial over a vast kickback scheme in the early 1990s. Construction companies are said to have paid €90 million (£63 million) in bribes to political parties in exchange for contracts to build and maintain secondary schools in the Paris area.[12]

Though it may seem a hopeful sign that justice is catching up with this era of corruption, albeit after a decade or more, the concept of corruption among French politicians has not changed. In January 2004 Alain Juppé, a former prime minister and close ally of the president, was convicted of being part of an illegal party funding scam. Far from shunning him, political colleagues applauded when he appeared back in parliament. President

---

11   www.euroaudio.dk/Triple_site/banns/manus_details.asp?UniqueID=512.
12   *Deutschewelle*, 26 March 2005,www.dw-world.de/dw/article/0,1564,1529624,00.
      html.

Chirac was glowing in his praise. 'He's a politician of exceptional quality – competent, humane and honest and France needs men of his quality.'[13]

The Elf slush fund

If individual donations to politicians and political parties are given overtly and are publicly recorded, this may be considered undemocratic because it places so much power in the hands of the wealthy, but it is not corrupt. If, however, donations above a legal threshold are made covertly, they become corrupt. Thus, the application for political purposes over many years by French presidents and others of a slush fund belonging to the then state-owned petroleum company Elf was clearly corrupt. Even in France, where corruption among politicians is cynically taken to be the norm, the discovery of Elf's slush fund in the late 1990s caused outright condemnation. During the 1980s and early 1990s the fund had been used for bribing officials in other countries and for political purposes, including contributions to Chancellor Kohl's Christian Democrat Party. The intention was to strengthen the Franco-German axis that for more than a decade had been attempting to dominate the EU. King (2004) gives a clear and depressing account of France's elite, who have been tainted with if not actually convicted of corruption since the mid-1980s. Jacques Chirac, Alain Juppé and François Mitterrand are some of the most notable.

Another detailed account of the corruption that is entrenched in France is given by Ignatius (2002). As executive editor of the

---

13   Ibid.

International Herald Tribune he chronicled the remarkable and courageous efforts of Eva Joly, an investigating magistrate, in unearthing a vast network of corruption at the highest political and business levels in France in the 1990s. Those whom she named and who were ultimately found guilty of corruption and other offences were: Roland Dumas, a former foreign minister; Charles Pasqua, former interior minister; and Bernard Tapie, a businessman with political friends everywhere, who was urban affairs minister, appointed by Mitterrand.

A key player in handling the Elf slush fund was Alfred Sirven, the head of Elf International in Switzerland and primary aide to Loïk Le Floch-Prigent, the head of Elf. It became clear that he was the crucial witness in the Elf case, but he fled France in 1997 and was eventually found in the Philippines. The French government arranged for his extradition to France in February 2001. As he was being captured Sirven swallowed the computer chip in his cell phone, so his telephone contacts while in exile have remained unknown. His address book was discovered, however, and published in *Paris Match*. Sirven's contact list included the private phone numbers of some of the most prominent politicians and business figures in France. When the Elf trial finally took place in January 2001 Sirven refused to testify.

Verdict: Silver medals for Roland Dumas, Charles Pasqua and Bernard Tapie. Bronze medals for Loïk Le Floch-Prigent and Alfred Sirven.

François Mitterrand
Although President Mitterrand died in 1996 the shadow of his

corruption has lived on for years and has become known as '*la Mitterrandie*'. In November 2004 nine former executives and state officials appealed against convictions for their part in the Elf oil company trial. The trial also exposed the way in which the presidency is financed by other organs of state. 'Its money escapes the auditors a little like the royal purse did,' said M. Ménage, who was Mitterrand's deputy chief of staff. At the trial Judge Kross voiced amazement that all staff at the Elysée had fictional jobs.[14]

Verdict: A gold medal to Mr Mitterrand, a silver medal for Mr Ménage, and nine bronze medals for the other participants (Loïk le Floch-Prigent's silver medal has already been awarded). The number of fictional jobs at the Elysée is not known so a token 100 nickel medals are awarded.

Alain Juppé

Alain Juppé was one of France's revolving-door prime ministers. In January 2004 he received an eighteen-month suspended prison sentence and was also barred from public office for ten years. The charges related to a jobs scam at Paris's City Hall while Mr Chirac was mayor. Seven staff working for their political party, then the Rally for the Republic (RPR), were put on the city hall's payroll. Mr Juppé said that while he had made mistakes, he had been 'stunned' by the court's verdict.

Verdict: As a one-time prime minister, Mr Juppé earns a gold medal.

---

14   Charles Bremner, *The Times*, 20 November 2004, p. 5.

Jacques Barrot, European commissioner

In November 2004 Nigel Farage, a British MEP, revealed that Jacques Barrot, who was nominated by France and is now vice-president of the European Commission, had been sentenced to an eight-month suspended sentence and was barred from elected office in France for two years in 2000 after being convicted of embezzling FFr25 million (£2.5 million) from government funds by diverting it into the funds of his party.

President Chirac subsequently granted M. Barrot a presidential amnesty, making it illegal under French law even to mention the conviction. Many MEPs were unaware of the conviction because it was censored in the French media.

Verdict: Embezzlement under my definition is stealing, not corruption. In the present case we cannot know how M. Barrot was able to divert funds because discussion of his case in the media has been suppressed in France. The facts, however, echo the general concept held in France that if money is diverted to a political party rather than to an individual, this is not corruption. Under my definition it is corruption because the favour goes to a nominee of the corruptor, in this case the UMP party. No medal is awarded.

President Jacques Chirac

During his long career in politics Jacques Chirac has been implicated in various scandals, but for the time being he is out of reach of prosecutors because of presidential immunity. He will remain immune until 2007 when his current term expires.

Allegations have been made that M. Chirac took kickbacks of

as much as £500,000 when he was mayor of Paris. The evidence is in the form of a videotaped confession by M. Jean-Claude Méry, a former official of the president's party and a member of its central committee. The allegations are made in an hour-long videotape, recorded at M. Méry's request by a freelance television producer, Arnaud Hamelin, in May 1996, and published in September 2000. M. Méry died in June 2000.[15]

M. Méry made the private video recording – allegedly for his own protection – when his role in corrupt funding of the RPR was under criminal investigation in 1996. In the transcript of the tape, published by the newspaper *Le Monde*, M. Méry alleges that he was receiving up to £4 million pounds a year in cash from companies working on public housing and schools for the Paris town hall for more than seven years up to 1996. On the tape he says this money was divided secretly between all the main French political parties, with the lion's share for M. Chirac's RPR and lesser payments to the Communist Party and the Socialist Party, whose first secretary was then Lionel Jospin, who later became prime minister. M. Méry goes on to allege, however, that one payment of FFr5 million (about £500,000) in cash in 1986 was 'paid directly' not to the RPR, but to M. Chirac, who was then prime minister as well as mayor of Paris.

Among other revelations, M. Méry describes a meeting in October 1986, when he visited Michel Roussin, the head of M. Chirac's private office at the Matignon Palace, the official residence and workplace of French prime ministers. He says that M. Chirac came to the meeting and was present in the room when he, M. Méry, placed FFr5 million in cash on M. Roussin's

---

15   John Lichfield, a writer with the *Independent*, published on 22 September 2002 at www.globalpolicy.org/nations/corrupt/governmt/Chirac.htm.

desk. M. Méry said the money came from kickbacks on heating contracts for public housing which had been awarded by the city of Paris to two large companies, Lyonnaise des Eaux and Générale des Eaux (now Vivendi). Was this money being 'paid directly' to the RPR? M. Méry asks himself on the tape. 'No – to Mr Chirac,' he replies.

Investigators believe that while Chirac was mayor of Paris in the 1990s he used substantial public funds to pay for personal vacations for himself, his family and his entourage. If correct, this would be stealing rather than corruption. M. Chirac has said, however, that the money came from a special fund he was entitled to use as prime minister between 1986 and 1988. Investigators are also looking into allegations that Paris City Hall, then under Mayor Chirac, received millions of francs in kickbacks in the 1980s and early 1990s and funnelled the money into his RPR party.

Verdict: Some commentators have described M. Méry's videotape as a smoking gun, while others have said that, because he is dead, the force of his evidence is weakened. In this case a gold medal is awarded because French legal systems offer presidential immunity and therefore make it impossible to establish truth. As is clear below, I regard this feature of legal systems to be unacceptable and a direct encouragement of the worst kind of corruption.

Lionel Jospin

In M. Jospin's case, it is inconceivable that as first secretary of the Socialist Party he could have been unaware of the origin of such substantial funds. It is much more likely that he took the French view that this was a normal way of funding political parties. Under my definition the money was a favour to Paris's City Hall for awarding contracts. In accepting money from this source M. Jospin and other political leaders were part of a process that conforms to my definition of corruption. As a later prime minister, M. Jospin is also awarded a gold medal.

Hervé Gaymard

In February 2005 *Le Canard Enchaîné*, the French satirical newspaper, reported that Hervé Gaymard, the finance minister, had rented a flat at £9,700 per month which was being paid for by the taxpayer. Was this corruption or theft?

In fact it may have been neither, although M. Gaymard resigned shortly afterwards, having been in office for only three months. If he was entitled to free accommodation as a perk of office, as are various British ministers, he was merely extravagant rather than corrupt. When the matter came to light, however, he agreed to repay all the expenses he had incurred on the short tenancy.[16] This suggests that he was claiming public funds to which he was not entitled. So far there has been no suggestion that the rent that he was expecting the treasury to pay represented a favour or a bribe for actions under his authority. It seems to be just a further example of how French politicians consider public office to be a means of self-enrichment.

Verdict: No medal is awarded to M. Gaymard.

---

16 Charles Bremner, *The Times*, 26 February 2005.

Germany: CPI rank 15

The Helmut Kohl era

Chancellor Helmut Kohl was Federal Chancellor for sixteen years and head of the CDU party for over twenty years. In 2000 evidence emerged that illegal secret campaign donations to his party had been common for many years. Kohl controlled the money, which was distributed within the party, often as cash in briefcases. The former Chancellor refused to reveal the donors' names. Using these funds, the CDU set up secret accounts in Switzerland and Liechtenstein.

In the late 1990s a different CDU financial scandal took place in the province of Hesse. Party officials were found to have about US$10 million (£8 million) in foreign bank accounts that may have been set up in the 1970s. Those responsible included Manfred Kanther, a former regional party chief who was interior minister in Kohl's government.

The Social Democrats (SDP), Germany's other big party, had similar scandals. A regional minister in North Rhine-Westphalia had to resign over a funding scandal and the prime minister of Lower Saxony also resigned over another incident.

The secret funds from donors to political parties appear to have gone to the parties themselves rather than as bribes to individual politicians. The covert donations to parties benefited politicians, however, who in turn had authority to benefit the corruptor in cases such as the sale of the Leuna chemical plant to Elf-Aquitaine in 1992 and the sale of 114,500 Deutsche Bahn apartments in 1998 at a figure below that offered by another bidder. It is clear that politicians' actions are likely to have been influenced by these illegal and covert donations. Key governmental files relating to some of the events disappeared.

Verdict: A gold medal for Helmut Kohl, silver medals for Kanther and for the Lower Saxony prime minister, and a bronze for the provincial minister.

Recent political corruption

Corruption is seen to be an increasing problem in Germany in both the political and private sectors. In August 2005 Ludwig-Holger Pfahls, a former junior defence minister under Helmut Kohl from 1987 to 1992, was jailed for two years and three months. He admitted receiving €2 million (£1.3 million) in bribes from an arms dealer, Karlheinz Schreiber.[17]

In January 2005 Jann-Peter Jansse, a member of the Bundestag (the lower house of the federal parliament), resigned. He had denied receiving undeclared money from Volkswagen (VW), but the company revealed that he had been on its payroll until the end of 2004. Five other Social Democrats were also listed by VW as paid employees.

Previously two prominent conservative politicians, the CDU's general secretary, Laurenz Meyer, and the party's labour affairs spokesman, Herman-Josef Arendtz, had been forced to resign after they admitted they had received undeclared payments from the giant energy company RWE. In an effort to prevent further revelations RWE admitted making secret payments to politicians of more than €600,000 (£420,000) each year for lobbying activities, mostly to local politicians. German politicians are allowed to have other jobs, but they are obliged to declare any outside employment to avoid conflicts of interest.[18]

---

17 *The Times*, 13 August 2005, p. 41.
18 *Deutschewelle*, 12 February 2005, www.DW-World.de.

Verdict: The junior minister Pfahls, general secretary Meyer and the labour affairs spokesman Arendtz are each awarded a silver medal. The Bundestag MPs earn six bronze medals.

Business corruption

At the time of writing Deutsche Bahn's chief executive, Hartmut Mehdorn, is being investigated by prosecutors in the German city of Neuruppin for possible corruption in relation to a ten-year contract worth €1.9 billion (£1.3 billion) awarded to Deutsche Bahn for subsidised passenger services on about 70 per cent of lines in Brandenburg – those that are most lucrative. The contract was negotiated by Hartmut Mehdorn and Hartmut Meyer, the latter then being the transport minister of Brandenburg. In September 2003, less than a year after the contract was signed, Meyer unexpectedly left his job at the ministry after ten years in office to become an adviser to Deutsche Bahn.

Verdict: When, immediately after leaving office, a minister takes a lucrative job in the private sector for which he was responsible, questions are bound to be asked, but the overtness of the move means that in itself it is not corrupt. No medals are awarded.

New Munich soccer stadium

In March 2004 Karl-Heinz Wildmoser was dismissed as head of the holding company building the €286 million (£188 million) Allianz Arena in Munich after an allegation that he took an illegal €2.8 million (£2 million) payment from an Austrian builder, Alpine, for inside information about the bidding process.

Wildmoser's father, also called Karl-Heinz, resigned as president of a local football club, TSV 1860 Munich, after being linked to the scandal.[19]

Verdict: Two nickel medals for the Wildmosers, father and son.

Fixing soccer matches[20]

In February 2005 a German soccer referee, Robert Hoyzer, admitted accepting bribes to manipulate matches. A total of 25 people are suspected of playing a part in rigging soccer matches with players, referees and outside parties involved.

Verdict: Robert Hoyzer wins a nickel medal and several more nickel medals may be in the pipeline. We award a provisional total of ten.

Greece: CPI rank =49

Tzilivakis (2003) gives an account of the efforts then being made by Greek politicians to root corruption out of the system. She gives instances of corruption cases involving planning permissions and building permits.

In 2000 the prime minister, Costas Simitis, personally congratulated an orthopaedic specialist for going to the authorities when his superior requested €5,870 (£4,100) to approve his application for a job transfer to the Social Insurance Foundation (IKA) branch in Corinth.

---

19   www.ESPNSoccernet.com, 30 November 2004.
20   *Deutschewelle*, 12 February 2005.

A poll by Kappa Research in January 2001 found that about 40 per cent of Greeks have witnessed corruption at least once. Surveys also show that the health sector is highly affected. For example, a *fakelaki* is a cash 'gift' for the doctor before an operation or medical treatment which is thought to guarantee the best possible care for a patient and a nicer room in public hospitals.

A bribe of several hundred euros is enough to be issued a driver's licence without taking the test. The construction business is also riddled with bribes and kickbacks. Architects, builders and employees at town planning offices all need 'hurry-up' fees to issue permits without delay. These fees can be up to €1,000 (£700).

Corruption is also rife in tax offices. In January 2003 the economy minister, Nikos Christodoulakis, announced that 80 tax collectors had been suspended on suspicion of accepting bribes and other perks.

Verdict: With corruption apparently rife at the lower levels of Greek institutions it is probable that higher levels are corrupt too. At present we award Greece a token 1,000 nickel medals for widespread low-level corruption.

Ireland: CPI rank =17

Charles Haughey

Charles Haughey was leader of the Fianna Fáil party and prime minister (Taoiseach) of Ireland four times. He officially retired in 1992. Renowned for his expensive tastes, in 2000 he was invest-igated by the Moriarty Tribunal on charges that during his career he received up to Ir£13 million (£13 million) in gifts and payments from wealthy businessmen.[21] Another minister, Michael Lowry, is also under investigation. Mr Haughey's health has been poor for some time and this has restricted his appearances before the tribunal.

The transcripts of some of the Moriarty Tribunal's hearings make it clear that significant sums of money were given to Mr Haughey by firms that had dealings with the government. Whether the money reached the Fianna Fáil's coffers or disappeared in private accounts is for the tribunal to resolve. Mr Haughey has been unable to explain the funding of his lavish lifestyle as a politician.

The Moriarty Tribunal consists of a single judge, Mr Michael Moriarty, who seems in no hurry to produce a report. From its start in 1997 to February 2005 it has cost €18.6 million (£13 million) and it still shows no sign of reporting.

The web of political bribery in Ireland seems to have been extensive. In January 2001 journalists watched a parliamentarian, Liam Lawlor, light a bonfire in his back garden to burn allegedly confidential financial documents. Mr Lawlor had just spent a week in Mountjoy Prison for refusing to cooperate with the Flood Tribunal, which investigated the planning process relating to land in County Dublin and improper payments made to politicians. Lawlor was allegedly at the centre of a web of bribery involving politicians that stretched back twenty years.[22]

Verdict: We award Mr Haughey a provisional gold medal which will be removed should the Moriarty Tribunal exculpate him of receiving money for favours granted.

---

21 http://news.bbc.co.uk/1/hi/northern_ireland/845446.stm.
22 Transparency International, *Global Corruption Report*, 2001.

In Mr Lawlor's case, burning documents does not of itself constitute corruption, but it means that there was something to hide. He receives a provisional bronze medal. More medals may be awarded when the Moriarty Tribunal reports.

Italy: CPI rank 42

Jones (2003) quotes Machiavelli's statement: 'We Italians are irreligious and corrupt above others ... because the Church and her representatives set us the worst example.' Does this hold good in my reference period of 1980 to the present?

There is still substantial evidence to support Machiavelli's reference to Italian corruption. According to Frei (2005) corruption in the 1980s reached the point where no contracts for public works were signed unless a substantial bribe (*tangente*) had been paid to the politicians involved. The naive assumption was that the recipients would pass the whole amount to their party. Even the communists, though they denounced such illegal payments, yielded occasionally to temptation by accepting them when the local administration was in their hands. Though this was supposedly a way of financing political parties, in practice much of the money stayed in the bank accounts of the corruptees concerned.

The result, Frei says, was that the Italian landscape became littered with unfinished motorways, unused canals, abandoned hospitals and building sites for projects whose completion had sometimes never been intended. This systematic extortion of funds through public contracts was as harmful as the 'protection money' that supported the Mafia. Both led to increased prices for consumers and losses to the government. Without these bribes the parties and politicians would have had to curtail lavish life-styles that they had come to take for granted.

Corruption in Sicily

In Sicily the dominance of the Mafia has provided a permanent link between corruption and organised crime. According to one source:

> entire economic sectors (hotels, transportation, banking, and construction) are controlled by Mafiosi. In a land without a tangible industrial base, public monies are the Mafia's main target. Everything has its price. Most politicians (whether liberal or conservative) can be bought, and the same holds true for the managers of banks and utilities. In Sicily many or most public or semi-public jobs are sold for money or sex. An attractive, smart but unemployed young woman is easy prey in a region with a 30 per cent unemployment rate. Public contracts are assigned (actually sold) in exchange for bribes and kickbacks. Everybody expects a substantial kickback, from the politician who gets you a public advertising or construction project to the event organiser who gets your musical group a gig in the local music festival. In business, money laundering is a way of life. In such a climate, the *pizzo* (protection money) and narcotics trades are little more than a side show.[23]

According to the same source, the regime of widespread if not universal corruption in Sicily is boosted by funds injected into the Sicilian economy by the World Bank, UN agencies, the USA and

---

23   www.bestofsicily.com/mafia.htm, 30 January 2005.

the European Commission, which have ended up in the hands of corrupt politicians, consultants and others connected with the Mafia. Bribery and kickbacks known as *bustarella* – from the Italian *busta*, an envelope – are normal.

Mainland Italy

There have been some important attempts at cleansing the system. In mainland Italy, 1992 saw the start of what became known as the Tagentopoli affair in Milan. A courageous judge, Antonio Di Pietro, and three other prosecutors began to unravel a web of systematic kickbacks that had influenced the awarding of service contracts on Milan's subway system, airport, railways, a soccer stadium, a theatre and other projects. Following a year of investigations they arrested or issued warrants for 70 people, including two former mayors, a billionaire industrialist and well-connected supporters of political organisations, predominantly the Italian Socialist Party. Their investigation, which became known as *mani pulite* (clean hands), began with the arrest of Mario Chiesa, a prominent socialist who ran Milan's best-known senior citizens' home and who was found to possess unreported funds totalling more than $11 million (£6 million). He gave information that incriminated others, including aides of Bettino Craxi, Italy's socialist prime minister from 1983 to 1987. Ultimately charges were brought against Craxi himself. In 1994 he was sentenced *in absentia* to eight and a half years in prison for accepting bribes, and in 1995 he received a further four-year sentence, also for corruption. Craxi avoided imprisonment by living in self-imposed exile in Tunisia.

Those who were being investigated, however, fought back by impugning the integrity and the political motivation of Di Pietro

Table 3 **Italy: statistics for legal action against corruption, 2000**

February 1992–March 2000*

Committals for trial requested	3,246
People convicted by the preliminary judge	581
People acquitted by the preliminary judge (181 were acquitted because of expiry under a statute of limitations)	444
People still before the preliminary judge	370
People indicted	1,234
People convicted by the court	576
People acquitted by the court (of which 124 because of a statute of limitations)	220
People before the court	438

Source: UNDP case study of corruption†
*The case study notes: 'because of the difference between the legal system in Italy and other countries it is difficult to explain these different categories precisely'.
†UNDP PARAGON Generic Training Model, op. cit.

and his colleagues. In December 1994 Di Pietro resigned amid widespread public consternation, for he had become the most popular man in Italy. He claimed that his position had become too politicised. His work continued, however, as shown in Table 3.[24]

Verdict: Bettino Craxi, as a former prime minister, wins a gold medal. In the absence of information about the job titles or positions of those convicted in Table 3 I award a token 250 bronze and 250 nickel medals. This will be an underestimate because of the number of cases that were quashed on account of a statute of limitations.

24 UNDP PARAGON Generic Training Module on Public Service Ethics and Accountabiltiy. Italy: G05B, http://unpan1.un.org/intradoc/groups/public/documents/eropa/unpan002688.pdf.

Cesare Previti

In November 2003 an Italian court sentenced a friend of Prime Minister Silvio Berlusconi to five years in jail for corruption. Cesare Previti, a former defence minister who had been on trial for three years, was convicted on charges of paying a $434,000 (£240,000) bribe to a Rome judge in 1991. He appealed but the verdict was upheld.

Verdict: A silver medal.

Silvio Berlusconi

On 13 July 1998 the BBC's online network reported: 'The former Italian Prime Minister Silvio Berlusconi has received his third conviction for corruption for making illegal payments to Italy's Socialist Party in 1991. A Milan court sentenced Mr Berlusconi to two years and four months' imprisonment, and gave him a fine of $6m … It is Mr Berlusconi's third prison sentence for corruption in the past seven months. He has already been convicted on one count of tax fraud and, in another case, of bribing tax inspectors. He faces six other criminal prosecutions for alleged bribery and false accounting.' The BBC's Rome correspondent stated that the legal process is so slow in Italy that these cases would be unlikely to conclude with Mr Berlusconi in prison, and some might fail because of a statute of limitations.

Since 1994 magistrates have investigated many allegations against Mr Berlusconi, including money-laundering, association with the Mafia, tax evasion, complicity in murder and bribery of politicians, judges and the finance ministry's police, the Guardia di Finanza. Mr Berlusconi, who denies all the allegations, maintains

87

that left-wing magistrates dominate the judiciary and that the *mani pulite* investigations were politically motivated.

In June 2003 Signor Berlusconi's majority party hurriedly passed a bill to grant legal immunity to himself as prime minister and to four other top state officials. This would have had the effect of freezing his trial for the rest of his term. In January 2004, however, the Italian constitutional court rescinded the new law. The hearings resumed but then stopped when the judge concerned decided that the matters at issue lay beyond his authority.

Berlusconi's relationship with Bettino Craxi deserves mention. For example, in October 1984 officials in several Italian cities shut down Berlusconi's television stations for broadcasting illegally. This spelled potential disaster for his heavily indebted Fininvest group. Within days, Craxi, who died in Tunisia after being sentenced *in absentia* to imprisonment for corruption, as noted, signed a decree that allowed Mr Berlusconi's stations to stay on air. After some parliamentary tussles, this decree became law.

In 1990 another law was passed that benefited Berlusconi. The Mammi Law, named after Oscar Mammi, the telecommunications minister, was enacted in 1990. It was tailor-made to suit Mr Berlusconi with his three national television networks and stipulated that no single group could own more than three out of the twelve networks that would be licensed. The coalition government of the day, which depended heavily on Craxi's Socialist Party, pushed through this controversial measure despite the resignation of five ministers in protest. In effect, this law entrenched the duopoly between Mediaset and RAI.

Verdict: Silvio Berlusconi earns a gold medal.

Luxembourg: CPI rank 13

An Internet search revealed no cases of corruption.

Verdict: No medals.

Netherlands: CPI rank 10

At a conference on corruption in May 2003, hosted by the Dutch government, the justice minister, Benk Korthals, included the following statement in his speech: 'The Netherlands, once so correct, has recently been scourged by fraud and corruption cases. The stock exchange, the Amsterdam municipal transportation company, the taxi world, the tax authorities, the police and even the Immigration and Naturalisation Service and the judiciary cannot escape accusations of corruption.'[25]

Despite this speech an Internet search did not reveal cases of the sort he was referring to.

Verdict: In the absence of tangible cases, I award the Netherlands no medals.

Portugal: CPI rank 27

This section draws largely on an undated but seemingly recent article by Rui Araújo on the website of the Center for Public Integrity, an institute in Washington, DC, whose mission is 'investigative journalism in the public interest'.[26]

In recent years corruption, both economic and moral, has

---

25 www.justitie.ne.

26 http://store.publicintegrity.org/ga/country.aspx?cc=pt&act=notebook.

surfaced alarmingly in Portugal. The foreign minister, Antonio Martins da Cruz, and the higher education minister, Pedro Lynce, resigned following a scandal involving the education of the former's eighteen-year-old daughter, Diana, who was given a place at Lisbon University to read medicine after Mr Lynce decided that she did not need to pass the entrance exams.

Verdict: Two silver medals.

The environment minister, Isaltino Morais, resigned in April 2003 after reports circulated that he had evaded taxes through undeclared accounts in Swiss banks.

Verdict: the evasion of taxes by a politician may be inadvisable but in itself it is not corrupt.

At lower municipal levels, notably among the traffic police, corruption is widespread. 'Portugal is drowned in a black tide of corruption,' Boaventura de Sousa Santos, a sociologist at Coimbra University, is quoted as saying. 'European funds, public works and soccer scandals are followed by those of security forces and paedophilia.'

In 2003 the mayor of a northern city, Fátima Felgueiras, escaped to Brazil, whence she protested her innocence on 30 counts of corruption, embezzlement, prevarication and abuse of power. She had been charged with managing a US$1 million (£800,000) *saco azul* (blue bag) to pay for her own electoral propaganda, the Socialist Party's office rent, phone bills and her new Audi. Seventeen other town hall employees and private entrepreneurs were involved in the inquiry. Police sources said the mayor escaped to Rio de Janeiro just before authorities received the warrant issued by the court. The police inquiry produced more than 120 volumes.

A Group of States Against Corruption (GRECO)[27] team that visited Portugal concluded that the most frequent forms of corruption are the acceptance or solicitation of bribes by public officials and bribery by entities outside government bodies. Over the past two years investigations have studied corruption in local government municipalities, branches of central government, the police, the tax authorities and clerks to the law courts. At other levels Republican National Guard officers, police officers, municipal employees, traffic authority personnel and occasionally judicial police have been widely reported over the illicit use of their positions to obtain financial benefits. Allegations of corruption have also been made against doctors, those who run auction rooms and sports officials.

Professor Jorge de Almeida Cabral of Universidade Lusófona has noted the exchange of favours between political parties and business.

Verdict: A provisional bronze medal is awarded to the ex-mayor, Fátima Felgueiras, who at the time of writing is protesting her innocence. Other bronze and nickel medals should be awarded in large numbers. A token 1,000 are divided between these two categories.

---

27   Founded in 1999 within the framework of the Council of Europe.

Spain: CPI rank =22 with France

The following cases of corruption are listed by Expatica.[28]

The ex-secretary of state for security, Rafael Vera, was jailed in October 2004 for seven years for paying out bonuses to personal contacts and stealing up to €5 million. He was ordered to pay back €3.9 million (£2.7 million) and he had three houses and property seized.

Verdict: A silver medal.

In 2001 the Gescartera brokerage house collapsed and its main shareholder, Antonio Camacho, was jailed after €108 million (£75 million) of clients' money went missing. He had used the money to pay for gifts and to buy jobs for staff at the Spanish stock market regulator, and pocketed the rest. One junior minister was forced to resign. Camacho served three years in prison. None of the €108million has been paid back.

Verdict: Camacho earns a bronze medal and the junior minister a silver medal.

In 1994 the director of the Guardia Civil, Luis Roldan, used his job to pay bribes and defraud the state of €60,000 (£42,000) each month. He fled Spain, and his easy escape forced the resignation of the then interior minister. Eventually captured, he claimed he took cash on the orders of government officials to fund the Socialist Party. He was jailed in 1998 for 28 years, later reduced to 20 years, for embezzlement, fraud and tax evasion. He was fined

---

28   www.expatica.com.

€13.1 million (£9 million) and so far he has paid off €3.6 million (£2.5 million).

Verdict: Roldan earns a silver medal. The interior minister may have resigned for incompetence rather than for complicity and so does not earn a medal.

In 1996 Luis Pascual Estevill, a judge in Barcelona, was jailed for nine years and fined €1.8 million (£1.3 million) after being convicted of leading the largest corruption racket discovered in the Spanish judicial system in 25 years. Estevill, who had been a member of the General Council of the Judiciary, was found to have accepted bribes and helped run an extortion racket between 1990 and 1994.

A former high-profile Catalan lawyer, Joan Piqué Vidal, was also sentenced to seven years in prison and fined €900,000 (£630,000) in relation to the case. The court found that Estevill and Piqué Vidal had used their positions to demand backhanders from businesses involved in lawsuits. The extortion allowed them to accumulate hundreds of thousands of euros in bribes over the four-year period. As part of the sentence, they were ordered to compensate victims with amounts ranging between €3,000 (£2,100) and €90,000 (£63,000). Several other people found guilty of participating in the scam, including Estevill's son, were fined and sentenced to up to one year in prison.

Verdict: Two bronze medals for Vidal and Estevill and a nickel medal for Estevill's son.

In 2000 Jesus Gil, former mayor of Marbella, and his successor,

Julian Munoz, were found guilty of stealing €360 million (£252 million) over nine years from the council. Phantom companies charged the council €30 million (£21 million) between 1991 and 1995. Gil, the one-time owner of Atletico Madrid FC, was said to have personally received €4.6 million (£3.2 million), siphoning the cash into the football club. He was jailed for six months for corruption. Munoz was ordered to pay back €24 million (£17 million) and his financial assets were seized.

Verdict: Two bronze medals.

Sweden: CPI rank 6

Submarines for Thailand
In December 2004 Henrik Westander, a veteran peace researcher, published a newspaper article accusing Kockums Shipyard of bribing political parties in Thailand in order to secure a big order. Kockums denounced the article as lies. When on a previous occasion Westander accused Bofors of doing the same thing in the early 1980s, however, he was proved right. Government ministers in India were forced to resign and Bofors lost its foothold in a lucrative market.

Verdict: A nickel medal is awarded for the 1980s case.

Liquor monopoly bribes
In February 2005 Systembolaget, the state-owned liquor monopoly, sacked 50 employees who were charged with taking bribes from suppliers. Twenty-two others named by the prosecu-

tors had already left the company. The employees were among 92 people charged by prosecutors after a two-year investigation into widespread bribes given by suppliers to store managers in exchange for having their products offered in Systembolaget outlets across the country. Investigators found that a majority of the bribes were cash gifts deposited into the employees' bank accounts, while some were also offered travel vouchers or complete vacations. The combined value of the bribes given in the period 2000–03 was about SKr1.2 million (£91,000). Divided between 72 employees, this amounts to about £1,300 each.

Verdict: 72 nickel medals.

United Kingdom: CPI rank 11

'Sleaze' was a prominent issue in the general election of 1997 that brought Tony Blair to power. It was a general term that covered MPs who took cash for asking parliamentary questions, politicians who cheated on their wives, and a minister, Jonathan Aitken, who received free hospitality in Paris without declaring it. Tony Blair promised that a New Labour government would be transparently clean. In fact there have been events that have tested whether this promise has been fulfilled. At the time of going to press the issue of loans for honours is topical and has not been resolved. Cases that have been concluded are now discussed.

The Bernie Ecclestone affair

In January 1997, before the general election, Bernie Ecclestone, the hugely wealthy owner of Formula One car racing, gave the Labour

Party £1 million. In October 1997, when Tony Blair had become prime minister, Ecclestone had a meeting at Number 10 Downing Street at which he lobbied the prime minister to abandon plans to ban the advertising of tobacco products, which at the time were major sponsors of Formula One teams. The meeting was noted by the prime minister's private secretary, a senior and independent functionary. One month later the government proposed that Formula One should be given special dispensation from the tobacco advertising ban. With the press taking a keen interest in what had occurred, the Labour Party returned the £1 million.

Verdict: A crucial factor is that the meeting was recorded by a senior functionary and therefore was on the record. Everything that a minister does or says in the presence of his civil servants is recorded and increasingly records can be called upon to attack or defend the minister in question. Undoubtedly Tony Blair and his Labour colleagues would have preferred that Mr Ecclestone's donation had remained unnoticed. It was given at a time before the Electoral Commission had been set up. If Labour Party officials alone had been present it would have been off the record (covert). In practice the meeting came to light through journalists asking questions, and the civil servant's notes were published.

The Lakshmi Mittal affair

In 2002 Lakshmi Mittal, an Indian-born steel-making entrepreneur, donated £125,000 to the Labour Party. A few weeks later Tony Blair personally signed a letter to Adrian Nastase, Romania's prime minister, commending Lakshmi Mittal's bid for Romania's failing steelworks. When this came to light Mr Blair defended himself, saying that Lakshmi Mittal owned a British company. In fact the British company, which is based in the City, comprises about 100 employees who control the company's fleet of five ships. It makes no steel at all in the UK and Mr Mittal's steel-making plants worldwide compete directly against the British steel industry.

Verdict: Lakshmi Mittal's donation was overt because it had to be declared under the new legislation. That being so, Tony Blair was either badly advised or extremely foolish to write a letter in Lakshmi Mittal's favour. The donation was transparent, and not corrupt.

Ministers and MPs
Jonathan Aitken: In 1992 Jonathan Aitken was the Conservative minister for defence procurement. He became involved with Said Ayas, an international arms trader with strong links to the Saudi government. In September 1993 a secret meeting took place in Geneva, but Aitken and his wife incurred a substantial bill in a Paris hotel where the meeting was originally to take place. The bill for the hotel was paid by Ayas and this was not declared by Aitken. Very publicly, at a specially called press conference, he denied that he had received this favour and sued the *Guardian* newspaper. When incontestable proof emerged that he was lying, his case collapsed and he admitted the truth. Later he was sent to prison for perjury and attempting to pervert the course of justice.

Verdict: Jonathan Aitkin is a borderline case. He received a covert favour, which was against rules of ministers' behaviour, but it has not been alleged that this favour influenced *actions* for which he had *authority*. He earns no medal.

Other ministers and MPs: In 1994 it was reported that Neil Hamilton, then minister at the Department of Trade and Industry, and Tim Smith, then junior minister for Northern Ireland, had received money and other favours from a lobbying company, Ian Greer Associates. The company was working for Mohamed Al Fayed, the owner of Harrods, who claimed that the MPs had asked parliamentary questions among other forms of lobbying at the behest of Ian Greer. The activities were stated to have taken place in 1987–89, when both politicians were backbench MPs. Tim Smith admitted the accusations and resigned. Neil Hamilton to this day denies them and has brought unsuccessful court actions to clear his name. In his report at the time Sir Gordon Downey, the Parliamentary Commissioner for Standards, said the evidence that Neil Hamilton received cash payments directly from Mr Al Fayed in return for lobbying services was 'compelling'.

Verdict: A bronze medal for Tim Smith.

Other Conservative MPs were caught up in the scandal. Sir Andrew Bowden was found to have given 'a positively misleading explanation' to ministers and officials when failing to declare his interest in dealings over the House of Fraser. Sir Michael Grylls was found to have deliberately misled a Commons select committee by understating commission payments he received. Michael Brown failed to register an introduction payment from Mr Greer in relation to US Tobacco.

On 10 July 1994 the *Sunday Times* published an article stating that David Tredinnick and Graham Riddick, two Conservative MPs, had both accepted £1,000 for tabling parliamentary questions. The journalist's telephone conversations with the two MPs had been taped. A further MP, Bill Walker, had agreed to put down a question with £1,000 being paid to a charity of his choice.

The matter was referred to a committee of the House of Commons which found that 'the offer of payment to table a question ... is not of the same character as the offer of payment for a Member's vote, and does not seem ... to fall into the definition of bribery ... nevertheless, such an offer if made and accepted ... is certainly dishonourable and damaging to the standing and reputation of Parliament'.

Verdict: Two bronze medals are awarded for accepting money to table questions. It is important to bear in mind that the fact that the actions were legal has no bearing on the application of my definition. Other law-makers were guilty of lying, which, though dishonourable, is not corrupt and does not satisfy my definition.

Two western European non-EU members
Norway: CPI rank 8

In June 2004 the Norwegian company Statoil was found guilty of using bribes to secure contracts in Iran and fined NKr20 million (£1.6 million).

Verdict: A nickel medal.

In 2003 the National Authority for Investigation and Prosecution of Economic and Environmental Crime cooperated with the US Department of Justice to investigate a payment of US$10,000 (£8,000) from a now defunct subsidiary of the Norwegian firm Veidekke into the London account of Uganda's former energy minister, Richard Kaijuka. The incident led to Kaijuka being given the choice of voluntarily resigning or being fired from his new post as a director of the World Bank.

Verdict: A nickel medal for Veidekke.

In January 2002 Haavald Heide Schjerven, the former head of UNICEF's Water and Sanitation section, was convicted of corruption in an Oslo court, sentenced to a five-and-a-half-year prison term and ordered to pay $1.6 million (£1.3 million) in compensation for accepting cash and cars in return for awarding contracts. Hans Petter Frisvold, co-defendant and chairman of Petron AS, was convicted of assisting in the fraud. He received a two-year prison term for bribing Schjerven with about $100,000 (£55,000) in return for receiving $3.1 million (£1.7 million) in contracts.

Verdict: Bronze medals for Schjerven and Frisvold.

Switzerland: CPI rank 7

General comments

Corruption appears to be at a low level in Switzerland. In January 1989 a single telephone call caused the resignation of a federal councillor, Mrs Elisabeth Kopp, who was the head of the Justice Department. When she learned that her husband, a businessman, was going to be investigated by the police for alleged money-laundering, she rang him from the department saying, 'They are on their way.' When this call was discovered, she immediately resigned. Mr Kopp was later cleared of all charges.[29]

Verdict: No 'favour' in the normal sense passed between Mr and Mrs Kopp, and it is unclear that either was corruptor or corruptee. The action was a telephone call, but there is no suggestion that Mrs Kopp sought to influence the investigation. No medal is awarded.

Iraqi oil for food scandal
Eleven Swiss oil-trading companies were named in a list published by Baghdad's daily paper *Al-Mada* in December 2004. They were investigated in a judicial inquiry launched by Switzerland's State Secretary for the Economy. Othmar Wyss, an official concerned, stated: 'The targeted companies ... would have paid bribes to the Iraqi regime to accede to oil contracts. Should it turn out that they were paid under the table, then we will enter into judicial proceedings against them for violation of the UN embargo.'[30]

Significantly, Mr Wyss makes the distinction between whether or not the money was paid 'under the table'. If the money was paid overtly to obtain the contracts and was part of the documentation, the companies avoid being corrupt under my definition and seemingly under that of Othmar Wyss also.

Verdict: At the time of writing bronze medals may be in prospect but cannot yet be awarded.

---

29   www.eda.admin.ch/sub_ecfin/e/home/docus/potent.html.
30   www.acepilots.com/unscam/archives/000700.html.

The EU's accession and candidate states

In 2005 Cyprus, the Czech Republic, Estonia, Hungary, Latvia, Lithuania, Malta, Poland, Slovakia and Slovenia joined the EU. States that had originally been expected to join in the first wave included Bulgaria and Romania, but these two, together with Croatia and Turkey, are still waiting as candidate states.

The extent of corruption in ten accession or candidate states is set out in detail in a 2002 report by the Open Society Institute.[31] It reveals that corruption in the form of the bribing of politicians and officials is commonplace and accounts for 1.4–3.2 per cent of firms' annual revenues, as shown in Table 4 below. Note that the states that were accession states when the Open Society Institute's study was undertaken differ from those that actually joined in 2005.

With evidence of such widespread corruption within accession or candidate states the award of medals becomes superfluous. It is clear that a yawning gulf exists between what is considered unacceptable in much of the EU-15 and what is considered normal in the accession states.

Africa

Corruption is endemic in Africa. The aim of becoming rich quickly has been the hallmark of politicians in Africa since independence. Itemising it country by country would be repetitive, time-consuming and ultimately pointless. One example is given here: that of a single recent president of Nigeria, the continent's most populous country and, thanks to its oil, a state that should be wealthy.

---

31   The Open Society Institute, *Monitoring the EU Accession Process: Corruption and Anti-Corruption Policy*, 2002.

Table 4 **EU accession states: average percentage of annual revenues paid in unofficial payments by enterprises to public officials, 2002**

	Bulgaria	Czech Rep	Estonia	Hungary	Latvia	Lithuania	Poland	Romania	Slovenia
Average	2.1	2.5	1.6	1.7	1.4	2.8	1.6	3.2	1.4

Source: Open Society Institute, 2002

President Sani Abacha ruled as a despot from 1993, when he led a military coup, to 1998, when he died in mysterious circumstances. During his five years in power political opponents died in prison and human rights abuses were condemned widely. Meanwhile he amassed wealth that has been put at $3 billion (£1.6 billion) and which was placed in private bank accounts in Europe and the Gulf.[32]

A point of interest here is that corruption as I define it is superseded when those in power can steal from the state without hindrance. As noted earlier, theft is different from corruption. Kleptocracy is an extreme form of theft. In essence, Sani Abacha simply stole £300 million a year for five years. The Nigerian government is still trying to recover these looted funds and Sani Abacha's family is fighting protracted lawsuits to retain the money.

Debt relief to the world's poorest countries has become fashionable, and in the summer of 2005 the G8's leaders drew up plans for debt relief. The countries concerned are shown in Table 5 overleaf. All but six are African countries. Their 2004 CPI ratings are also shown: 0 is the lowest rating, meaning totally corrupt; 10 is the highest rating, which would be given to completely uncorrupt countries.

---

32 http://people.africadatabase.org/en/profile/1992.html.

Table 5 **Countries scheduled for debt relief and their CPI rating, 2004**

Country	CP Index 2004	Country	CP Index 2004
Debt to be dropped immediately			
Benin	3.2	Mozambique	2.8
Bolivia	2.2	Nicaragua	2.7
Burkina Faso	n/a	Niger	2.2
Ethiopia	2.3	Rwanda	n/a
Ghana	3.6	Senegal	3
Guyana	n/a	Tanzania	2.8
Honduras	2.3	Uganda	2.6
Madagascar	3.1	Zambia	2.6
Mali	3.2	**Average**	**2.8**
Mauritania	n/a		
Debt to be dropped in 18 months			
Cameroon	2.1	Guinea-Bissau	n/a
Chad	1.7	Malawi	2.8
Democratic Republic of Congo	2	São Tomé	n/a
Gambia	2.8	Sierra Leone	2.3
Guinea	n/a	**Average**	**2.3**
Debt to be dropped in future			
Burundi	n/a	Burma	n/a
Central African Republic	n/a	Somalia	n/a
Ivory Coast	2	Sudan	n/a
Laos	n/a	Togo	n/a
Liberia	n/a		

Sources: *The Times*, 13 June 2005, p. 32, and Transparency International

All the countries scheduled for debt relief have a poor rating for corruption. Those that are due for immediate debt relief are slightly less corrupt (average CPI = 2.8) compared with those due to receive relief in eighteen months' time (average CPI = 2.2). It would be nice to think that the leaders of the rich nations had tilted the balance slightly in favour of countries that are somewhat less corrupt than others. It seems likely, however, that a significant part of the debt to be written off has been spent not just on mismanaged investment projects but also on lining the pockets of corrupt rulers over many decades.

Some other states

A number of non-European states deserve attention. Australia, Canada, Japan and the USA are industrialised states with well-established traditions of democracy which might be expected to have low levels of corruption. China and Russia are major states with little tradition of democracy and so might be expected to have more corruption.

Australia: CPI rank 9

At the time of going to press a major scandal is being investigated by the Cole Commission in relation to the sale of wheat by the Australian Wheat Board (AWB) to Saddam Hussein's regime under the oil-for-food programme. Central to the inquiry is why AWB, Australia's sole wheat exporter, paid A$300 million (£128 million) in bribes by charging Iraq above-market prices to supply wheat. The extra cash was placed in a separate account which was allegedly used to bribe Iraqi officials. Damning evidence has been put to the inquiry by Mark Emons, AWB's former Middle East manager, who stated that the payment of bribes via 'trucking fees' was a common practice and had been taking place for years with the knowledge of senior management, including the then chairman, Trevor Flugge.[33] On his first day on the witness stand in March 2006 Mr Flugge is reported as having used the phrases 'I

---

33   *The Times*, 6 February 2006, p. 29.

can't recall', 'I don't remember' and 'my recollection doesn't take me there' almost 50 times.[34]

Verdict: This case has yet to reach a conclusion. Medals will be awarded if guilt is established.

In March 2004 the opposition Labour Party accused the federal government of a cash-for-comment bribe to regional newspapers as part of a secret AU\$3.25 million (£1.4 million) campaign to create public support for selling off Telstra, Australia's telephone provider. The opposition communications spokesman, Lindsay Tanner, said leaked government documents outlined a major media campaign under which the government would pay for full-page advertisements in exchange for stories based on information supplied by the government's Communications Department.

The influence of government and other big advertisers over the press is a grey area for potential corruption. The press worldwide is heavily dependent on advertising. If the government can buy favourable editorial stories in return for advertisements paid for from taxes, the distortion of democracy is self-evident. The advertisements are, however, overt by definition.

On the other hand, if the government of the day obtains editorial favours from the press in return for the advertisements, this is corrupt.

Verdict: The charge of corruption would be warranted if a secret deal between the government as corruptor and the press as

---

34   News.com.au, www.news.com.au/story/0,10117,18389219-421,00.html.

corruptee were proved. No medal can be awarded simply on the suspicion that this may have occurred.

Canada: CPI rank 12

The general election of January 2006 saw a big swing from the Liberals to the Conservatives, who won the largest number of seats in parliament though without an overall majority. Allegations of corruption were levelled against the former Conservative administration and were widely believed to have influenced the electorate. At the heart of the issue was an inquiry headed by Judge John Gomery about how and why C\$100 million (£43 million) were funnelled to advertising firms sympathetic to the Liberal Party, under a programme intended to sponsor national unity in the 1990s. Canada's auditor-general had concluded that little or no work was performed and the money was largely unaccounted for. At least one witness testifying to Judge Gomery said that some of the contracts concerned came from the prime minister's office and that the advertising firms had paid kickbacks to the Quebec section of the Liberal Party.

Judge Gomery reported in October 2005. He found that a select group of advertising firms in Quebec received lucrative federal contracts and then knowingly kicked back some of the money to the Liberal Party's Quebec wing, enabling it to sidestep electoral financing laws. He called it a 'blatant misuse of public funds'. He said that while there was no evidence that Mr Jean Chrétien, who was the Liberal prime minister when the payments were made, was aware of the kickback scheme, 'good intentions are not an excuse for maladministration of this magnitude'. Mr Chrétien ran the programme from his own office and as such was responsible for 'the defective manner' in which the programme's initiatives were implemented. Paul Martin, the Liberal finance minister at the time, was not implicated by Judge Gomery but, having succeeded Mr Chrétien as prime minister, was punished by the electorate in January 2006 when the Liberal Party lost power, and he resigned as the party's leader.

Verdict: Judge Gomery held that Mr Chrétien was incompetent rather than corrupt.

Other senior politicians and functionaries were caught up in the inquiry. Don Boudria was minister of public works for five months. He was removed from the post after it was revealed that he had stayed at a luxury chalet belonging to the owner of Groupe Everest, a Quebec firm that earned millions of dollars in business with the government.

Verdict: A silver medal for Don Boudria.

Jean Brault was the president and founder of Groupaction Marketing, one of the Quebec advertising agencies implicated in the scandal. He pleaded guilty on 2 March 2006 to five fraud-related charges and will proceed to trial on one charge of conspiracy.

Verdict: A bronze medal.

Paul Coffin was head of Communication Coffin, a Montreal advertising company. The company handled sponsorship deals on behalf of Public Works Canada between 1997 and 2002, worth $3.4 million. He pleaded guilty to defrauding the government.

Verdict: A bronze medal.

Benoît Corbeil was formerly the director general of the Liberal Party of Canada's Quebec wing. He was a key organiser in funnelling sponsorship money to the Quebec wing of the Liberal Party of Canada. Justice Gomery said that Corbeil accepted cash donations and improper benefits for the Quebec wing of the Liberal Party of Canada and 'contributed to the all too common perception that many of those participating in the democratic exercise of political activism are dishonest and disreputable'.

Verdict: A silver medal.

Alfonso Gagliano was a political organiser and a close friend of former prime minister Jean Chrétien. He was in charge of the Ministry of Public Works at a time when it was spending hundreds of millions of dollars promoting Canada in Quebec. When the scandal first broke Chrétien responded by removing Gagliano from the cabinet and making him ambassador to Denmark. The Paul Martin government fired him as ambassador. Gagliano denies having any knowledge of inappropriate commission fees being paid out by the ministry and on 27 May 2005 he filed a lawsuit against Paul Martin and his government for wrongful dismissal.

Verdict: It seems remarkable that Mr Gagliano should have no knowledge of what was being done by his ministry, but no medal can be awarded.

Chuck Guité was a senior functionary in the Ministry of Public Works. In a report by the auditor-general he was accused of breaking 'just about every rule in the book' when he worked on the sponsorship programme. Police have charged him with several counts of fraud. He has denied breaking the rules but admitted that 'We've bent them a little bit based on the circumstances'. He was referring to the way contracts were awarded without the usual competitive bidding process. He told a Commons committee that his political bosses, including then prime minister Jean Chrétien's chief of staff, Jean Pelletier, directed him to use certain advertising agencies when awarding sponsorship contracts.

Verdict: The traditional defence of 'I was only obeying orders' is still to be tested in the courts. No medal is awarded.

China: CPI rank 71

The penalties for corruption in China are severe, including long terms in prison or even the death penalty.

In August 2004 Bi Yuxi, head of the Capital Road Development Corporation and a deputy director of the Beijing City Transport office, was expelled from the Communist Party for 'degenerate' behaviour. According to the *Youth Daily* he accepted several huge bribes.

Verdict: Information emanating from dictatorial regimes such as China must be treated with caution, not least because of the absence of a free press. Bi Yuxi earns a silver medal.

In March 2005 a regulation issued by the Communist Party's publicity department and the State Administration of Radio, Film and Television stated that journalists face 'severe penalties' for corruption and false reporting. Seemingly the new regulation follows a scandal involving eleven journalists who allegedly took bribes in return for under-reporting the casualty figures in a mine blast in central Shanxi province.

Verdict: Eleven nickel medals.

In 2001 Jiang Yanping, a former deputy general manager of the Provincial Architectural Engineering Group of Hunan, was convicted of taking over US$1.2 million (£660,000) in bribes and sentenced to death.

Verdict: As Jiang's position was that of a business manager, a nickel medal is awarded.

Japan: CPI rank 24

In an account of corruption in Japan, Mitchell (1996) gives copious detail concerning the corruption that has been the hallmark of Japanese politics for 1,400 years. Here I focus on more recent cases.

The Recruit scandal, 1989

The Recruit company was found to have been giving large sums of money to influence politicians and senior functionaries in central government agencies. Prime Minister Takeshita Noboru and a former prime minister, Yasuhiro Nakasone, resigned. Finance Minister Miyazawa Kiichi, Justice Minister Hasegawa Takashi and Harada Ken, director general of the Economic Planning

Agency, also resigned. Kato Takashi, a vice-minister in the Labour ministry, was tried and found guilty.

Verdict: Two gold medals for the prime ministers; three silver medals for ministers and a silver medal for the head of a government agency.

The Tokyo Sagawa Express Company, 1992

The Tokyo Sagawa Express Company spread its largesse widely. It gave donations to about 130 Diet members, among them Kanemaru Shin, vice-president of the Liberal Democratic Party. He resigned from the Diet and in 1993 his home and office were searched while television cameras recorded the proceedings. Viewers witnessed the discovery of tens of millions of dollars in gold, cash and bonds. It seemed that the hoard was for personal rather than political use.

Verdict: 130 bronze medals.

The Financial Reconstruction Commission scandal, 2002

In August 2000 the *Asahi Shimbun* newspaper reported that the Financial Reconstruction Commission's chairman, Kimitaka Kuze, had accepted up to ¥210 million (£1.1 million) in advisory fees from the Mitsubishi Trust and Banking Group between 1983 and 1996 and that he was offered ¥100 million (£476,000) in 1991 by the construction company Daikyo. Within days he had been forced to resign.[35]

---

35   www.wsws.org/articles/2000/aug2000/jap-a01.shtml, 26 January 2005.

Verdict: Mr Kuze is awarded a silver medal.

The Takao Koyama affair, 2001
Prosecutors arrested Takao Koyama, a member of the Upper House for the ruling Liberal Democratic Party (LDP), over allegations that he accepted more than ¥20 million (£100,000) in bribes from an industrial insurance provider, KSD. The scandal forced the resignation of Masakuni Murakami as head of the LDP group in the Upper House. Prosecutors suspect that Koyama received the cash in 1996 from KSD in return for asking questions in parliament that were advantageous for the insurer. Koyama's involvement was widely seen as the tip of the iceberg of a scandal involving many more LDP law-makers. He resigned shortly after his arrest.

Verdict: Two bronze medals.

Unreported payments to Japanese members of parliament, 2005[36]
In January 2005 the *Japan Times* reported that a faction of the LDP, currently led by former prime minister Yoshiro Mori, provides its elected members with funds. Details of the money were not included in the group's funding reports from 1998 to 2003. In their first or second terms Diet members are typically given ¥2 million (£10,000), while those in their third or fourth term receive ¥1 million (£5,000). This is a long-established practice among major LDP factions by which factional leaders maintain the allegiance of

36   *Japan Times*, 23 January 2005.

their members through payment. Several law-makers belonging to the Mori faction confirmed to *Kyodo News* that they received funding support from the faction. The Political Funds Control Law stipulates that revenue such as donations and expenditures exceeding ¥50,000 (£250) must be declared.

In 2004, the LDP's biggest faction came under fire for false reporting of political funds, and former prime minister Ryutaro Hashimoto stepped down as head of the group. The faction's accountant was convicted for failing to report ¥100 million (£50,000) that the faction received in 2001 from the Japan Dental Association.

Verdict: The practice whereby individual Diet members receive payments from their political party or faction to ensure their loyalty seems to be a curious form of democracy, but provided that the payments are accurately and publicly reported they are not corrupt. When false reporting is involved, however, it follows that some part of the payments was concealed and thus were covert. Under my definition former prime minister Ryutaro Hashimoto earns a gold medal for this reason.

Corrupt officials

In 1997 150 government officials were under arrest for taking bribes. Eighty of these were local government officials, 50 were assembly members of local government, ten were police officials and ten were in the National Tax Administration.[37]

---

37   T. Hasegawa, www.unafei.or.jp/english/pdf/PDF_rms/no56/56-36.pdf 25 January 2005.

Verdict: On the simplifying assumption that these were lower-ranking people, 150 nickel medals are awarded.

NHK public service radio station

In March 2005 Katsumi Isono, the chief producer at NHK, the public service radio station, pleaded guilty to spending ¥2.7 million (£13,500) of NHK's money in 2001 to pay an event-planning firm for scripts that were never written. He received ¥1.8 million (£9,000) in kickbacks.[38]

Verdict: A bronze medal is awarded to Mr Katsumi.

Russia: CPI rank 90

The period from 1980 to the present covers the collapse of the Soviet Union of which Russia was the cornerstone. Martirossian (2004)[39] describes how corruption was rampant in the Soviet Union though officially accorded zero tolerance. Corruption was closely associated with the 'shadow economy' or black markets that came into being to deal with the endemic shortages of goods and services under the centrally planned economy.

Although Russia in some ways is now a liberal market economy, in other ways little has changed. Martirossian cites how entry to higher education institutions was restricted under the Soviet Union to 20 per cent of high school graduates. As a result many parents used bribes to the administrators to enable

---

38   *Japan Times*, 10 March 2005.
39   For much of the factual material in this section I am indebted to Martirossian (2004).

their children to gain places. She adds: 'It is remarkable that ... this corrupt practice continues unabated, even though in the new economy there are numerous private institutions of higher education.' Entrance to the state institutions is sought because those schools continue to enjoy high levels of prestige and tuition is either free or is provided at reduced fees. In other words the market for higher education remains distorted and paying bribes for student entry continues to reflect this.

The Soviet system of planning and targets that were never attained gave rise to *blat*, which meant the use of personal influence to obtain favours and supplies. Despite the state's official view about the unacceptable nature of *blat*, bribes and corruption became the only means of survival and hence acceptable in citizens' eyes. They have remained so since the fall of communism.

The corrosive effect of corruption becoming universal in Russia was that it infected the legal system also: 'Law was viewed not as a tool for serving justice but as a mechanism for personal enrichment ... Entry into the law departments of higher institutions of learning in the Soviet Union commanded one of the highest unofficial entrance fees (i.e. bribes or in-kind considerations) because of the promise of high earnings in the future.'

Post-Soviet Russia 'has been characterized by a massive tidal wave of corruption and organized crime' (ibid.: 88). Martirossian quotes Shelley (1997), who states that organised crime is so pervasive and oppressive that it is itself the new authoritarianism. It has supplanted weak government structures that at best were unable to fight organised crime and at worst colluded with it. The gun rules: of 1,800 people murdered in Moscow in 1997, nearly a third were the victims of contract killers who were almost never caught.

In terms of corruption, according to Russia's Interior Ministry 53,000 crimes were committed by government officials alone in 1999 – an increase of 36 per cent over 1998. Corrupt politicians and functionaries as well as crooked businessmen and organised crime syndicates are left alone by the police and prosecutors.

Yeltsin, Putin and Skuratov

When Boris Yeltsin handed over to Vladimir Putin on New Year's Eve, 1999, the latter's previous job was as head of the FSB, Russia's successor to the KGB. Of his 24 high-level appointments, ten went to former FSB and KGB colleagues. His first official decree granted immunity to President Yeltsin and his family. This was helpful to Yeltsin because Yuri Skuratov, the prosecutor-general of the Russian Federation, had been investigating capital flight out of Russia in which Yeltsin, his family and inner circle were heavily implicated. In April 2000 Skuratov was removed from office.

Putin, like his predecessors, has passed anti-corruption decrees but they have had no effect. They focus on the detection of corruption rather than its punishment and they encroach on personal privacy and individual rights. There is no witness protection programme to encourage whistle-blowing.

Verdict: Russia is a country in which corruption is so widespread that the award of medals would be futile.

United States of America: CPI rank 17

Political funding

According to Johnson (2004), in San Francisco there is an

assumption of a direct relationship between the money you donate to politicians and the city contracts you can expect to get. San Francisco politics are not that different from politics in other American cities, he claims. The justification for this practice is that politicians need large sums for their campaigns, and if contributions are made in accordance with rules, America's political money chase is not considered corrupt. In the context of my definition of corruption, if a payment to a politician or to a party is made *overtly*, that is to say if it is publicly declared to the authorities, the transaction is not corrupt. American law and culture support this view. The transparency of the donations that corporations and wealthy individuals give to politicians is an accepted feature of democracy in the USA.

The legal limit for donations per donor in California is $21,200 (£11,550), but there is no limit on donations to committees formed to promote individual measures that appear on the Californian ballot. Rich individuals can, of course, finance their own campaigns. Arnold Schwarzenegger spent $10 million (£5.5 million) on his campaign to replace Governor Gray Davis. The USA is used to seeing millionaire politicians being elected, and it could be argued that rich politicians are more likely to be independent than poor politicians who are financially dependent on the lobbies who pay for their election.

Government bureaucracy in the USA is seen as operating in a more entrepreneurial and pragmatic way than in Europe. There is a spoils system under which incoming politicians replace senior functionaries in the public service with their own people. Clearly this makes the appointees loyal to those who have appointed them but it does not make them corrupt. Most observers do not see corruption in the professional public service as widespread.

Politicians

Has the USA experienced corruption at high political level? Richard Nixon was a dishonest president but not corrupt under my definition. By contrast his vice-president, Spiro T. Agnew, was charged with, among other things, accepting bribes, and he resigned on 10 October 1973. Both Nixon and Agnew, however, lie outside my time frame.

The presidency of Bill Clinton will be remembered in the popular mind for the Monica Lewinsky affair. He may also be remembered for the remarkable presidential pardons that he announced on the last day of his presidency on 20 January 2001. Among others he pardoned Marc Rich, a businessman who had been in exile in Switzerland accused of rigging oil prices and avoiding taxes. Marc Rich had made financial contributions to Bill Clinton's presidential library, the Democratic Party and to Hillary Clinton's Senate campaign. This was not corrupt because it was overt. In leaving the pardon to his last day in office it is possible that Clinton thought he could minimise its newsworthiness.

Vice-President Dick Cheney has been in politics for many years, starting in Richard Nixon's era. From 1995 to 2000 he was head of Halliburton, an oil and gas engineering conglomerate that is the subject of an investigation into $180 million (£97 million) that may have been used by Halliburton as bribes to build a gas liquefaction plant in Nigeria. Gaining overseas contracts through bribery has been illegal for over 30 years in the USA and carries heavy penalties. Enquiries by the Securities and Exchange Commission in Washington, DC, and also by Renaud Van Ruymbeke, a renowned investigating magistrate in France, are in progress.

Verdict: If Dick Cheney is found to have authorised or known about bribes, the repercussions will be huge, and it seems likely that he would resign as vice-president. The allegation has not, however, been proven.

In October 2005 Tom DeLay was forced to resign as the Republican leader in the House of Representatives, having being charged with criminal conspiracy after a number of recent sleaze allegations.[40] Mr DeLay, a former cockroach exterminator, was known as 'The Hammer' because of his ruthless effectiveness in getting President Bush's domestic legislation through the House of Representatives. In 2004 the House Ethics Committee admonished Mr DeLay for trying to win a congressman's support for a key vote by offering tens of thousands of dollars to support his son's political future and over cash-for-legislation allegations. Both these are corrupt by my definition and the committee's leniency towards Mr DeLay at the time seems remarkable.

Verdict: A bronze medal for Mr DeLay.

At the time of writing a further major corruption scandal is emerging in Congress. In November 2005 Randy 'Duke' Cunningham resigned from the House of Representatives. A Republican congressman since 1991 and a member of the House Defense Appropriations Committee, he admitted accepting $2.4 million (£1.4 million) in bribes from defence contractors.

Worse seems to be in prospect with a criminal investigation by the Department of Justice into a Republican lobbyist, Jack

---

40　This section draws on *The Times*, 29 September 2005, p. 24.

Abramoff, who allegedly gave congressmen millions of dollars in donations in return for legislative favours on behalf of his clients. In December 2005 Michael Scanlon, his business partner, pleaded guilty to conspiring to bribe public officials. He is thought to have agreed to provide prosecutors with evidence that politicians took bribes in exchange for favourable votes. More than 30 members of Congress are alleged to have taken legislative action favourable to Mr Abramoff's clients after receiving money from the lobbyist and his clients. Most are Republican, but they include two Democrat senators.[41]

Verdict: Randy Cunningham earns a bronze medal and Michael Scanlon a nickel medal. It seems likely that up to 30 more bronze medals may be awarded.

Corporate corruption

At corporate level the scandals that began with the collapse of Enron in 2001 have tarnished corporate America with the perception of corruption, but is this justifiable? The sharp accounting practices that should have been stamped on by Andersen, the now defunct auditor, may have been contrary to accounting rules, and if they permitted individuals to take money from company funds, that was theft rather than corruption. Corruption as such would be the charge only if Enron covertly paid Andersen super-normal fees in order to conceal losses or white-collar theft by its employees.

Enron is in liquidation. Successful prosecutions with prison

---

41 *The Times*, 10 December 2005, p. 55.

sentences and fines have been achieved against some of its senior executives and other cases are in progress. These appear to relate to fraud and theft rather than corruption.

Verdict: No medals.

Marsh & McLennan, owned by MMC, describes itself as the world's leading risk and insurance services firm. The New York Attorney General's Office discovered that Marsh's executives allotted their clients' business on the basis of the kickbacks that the underwriters paid them instead of by which firms offered their clients the best cover. Marsh was accepting covert favours to influence transactions over which it had authority. This was corrupt.

In October 2004 the president and chief executive of MMC, Jeffrey W. Greenberg, was dismissed and five directors were replaced. In January 2005 MMC settled out of court with the New York Attorney General's Office and with the New York State Insurance Department by setting up a fund of US$850 million (£460 million) to compensate policy-holders over a four-year period.[42]

Verdict: MMC is a large corporation. I award bronze medals to Jeffrey Greenberg and the five board members who were dismissed.

---

42   MMC annual report, 2004, p. 7.

The medals table

Results

In summarising the results of this chapter in the medals table below, I stress that it is a snapshot of the tips of the corrupt icebergs in the countries and institutions concerned. Table 6 also enables a comparison to be made with the index numbers of the CPI 2004 for the countries in the table.

The countries included in the table account for about one third of the world's population. I have excluded regions such as Africa and individual states such as Russia where corruption is so endemic as to make awarding medals pointless. The table is not intended to be a comprehensive list of all relatively uncorrupt states, so a country that does not appear in the table should not automatically be taken as corrupt or indeed uncorrupt.

The tips of icebergs in my medals table cannot accurately reflect or compare the full extent of corruption below the waterline. Nevertheless, the table represents a new insight into corruption internationally and has the merit of being based on a robust definition that is independent of time, place, local laws and customs.

Conclusions

The rankings in Table 6 follow from the number of gold, silver, bronze and nickel medals awarded above. France heads the table with four gold medals followed by Japan with three and Italy with two. Germany, Belgium and Ireland follow with one each.

The table's rankings produce a reasonable concordance with the CPI's ranking and index values for the countries concerned. (China is an exception to this, but the lack of a free press prevents

Table 6 **Corruption medals table for the period 1980–2005**

Pop M		CPI 2004		Medals			
		Rank	Value	Gold	Silver	Bronze	Nickel
61.5	France	22	7.1	4	5	2	100
127.8	Japan	24	6.9	3	5	138	150
57.3	Italy	42	4.8	2	1	250	250
82.5	Germany	15	8.2	1	3	7	15
10.4	Belgium	17	7.5	1	2		
4.0	Ireland	17	7.5	1		1	
41.6	Spain	22	7.1		3	5	1
10.4	Portugal	27	6.3		2	501	500
31.8	Canada	12	8.5		2	2	
	European Commission				1	25	
1,280.4	China	71	3.4		1		12
	UN Secretariat				1		
291.0	USA	17	7.5			8	1
60.3	UK	11	8.6			3	
8.9	Sweden	6	9.2			2	73
4.6	Norway	8	8.9				2
11.0	Greece =	49	4.3				1,000
	Average	**24.0**	**7.1**				
	No medals						
20.0	Australia	9	8.8				
8.1	Austria	15	8.4				
5.4	Denmark	3	9.5				
5.2	Finland	1	9.7				
0.4	Luxembourg	13	8.4				
16.2	Netherlands	10	8.7				
7.3	Switzerland	7	9.1				
	Average	**8.3**	**8.9**				

Notes: Where a large rounded number such as 100 or 1,000 is given, this represents an extensive but unquantifiable number of cases. Countries with no medals are listed in alphabetical order.
Table: Ian Senior

Comments to be read in conjunction with the text

A token 100 nickel medals for fictional jobs in the Elysée

250 bronze and 250 nickel medals are token numbers based on official statistics, 2002
10 provisional nickel medals are awarded to football referees and others Agusta affair
Charles Haughey's gold medal is provisional

Many medals pending OLAF's investigations
Lack of a free press makes figures unreliable

The nickel medals are a token award for extensive low-level corruption

A corruption inquiry is in progress into the Australian Wheat Board

In 2003 justice minister said there was considerable low-level corruption in Netherlands important cases coming to light.) This concordance is confirmed by the averages for the group with medals, compared with averages for the group with none. Overall, the countries that win medals are found by the CPI 2004 to be more corrupt. Thus, the two entirely different methods of measuring corruption prove consistent.

3 CAUSES OF CORRUPTION

Introduction

The literature on the causes of corruption is voluminous but remarkably thin in terms of useful analysis. The first volume of Williams (2000) is titled *Explaining Corruption*, yet, as noted earlier, eighteen of the 28 papers do not define corruption. Authors throughout the volume extensively describe activities they believe to be corrupt. The discussion of causes centres on the obvious possibilities for corruption that are created when public officials have authority to award contracts and licences, to issue fines, assess taxes or just speed up actions their job requires them to do anyway. Less attention is paid to other possible causes.

By contrast, using stated hypotheses and independent data I have applied regression analysis to evaluate what may be the causes of corruption. The value of regression analysis is that it permits a large number of variables and large data-sets to be analysed to show which independent variables significantly affect or are correlated with the dependent variable and which do not. It does not matter how many independent variables are regressed at the same time provided that they are uncorrelated with each other. Regression then identifies those independent variables that *significantly* – which means in a statistically defined measure – relate to variations in the dependent variable.

English does not have direct antitheses to the noun 'corruption' or to the verb 'to corrupt' but I need them so, as readers will already have noted, I extend the English language with the following opposites: 'uncorrupt' (adjective or verb) and 'uncorruption' (noun).

Corruption, the dependent variable

In seeking data for the dependent Y variable, by far the best source of comparative international information concerning corruption comes from Transparency International (TI). Founded in 1993, TI states as its mission to combat corruption in all its forms worldwide. Its Corruption Perceptions Index (CPI), compiled at the University of Passau, Germany, is widely regarded as the most dependable available source for comparing corruption between countries internationally. It draws from twelve different independent sources on the extent of perceived corruption in the countries covered, and individual countries are included only if a minimum of three sources are available.

The 2004 index covered 146 countries. The CPI produces an index number for each country between 0 and 10. Zero means completely corrupt, ten means completely uncorrupt. The CPI, namely *perceived* corruption, is the dependent variable in my model and is a proxy for *actual* corruption, which because it is covert cannot be measured except in isolated cases, such as those given earlier, when particular corruption trials bring actual values into the public domain.

The fourteen independent variables

My choice of the independent variables (the X variables) began with my looking for data with which to test hypotheses that seemed intuitively likely. Inevitably the data I found came from several sources, all of which are referenced. I found fourteen data-sets that appeared robust and which covered independent variables that intuitively seemed worth including in the model.

The available data-sets did not cover all the countries found in the CPI. As multiple regression requires an observation for every country and every variable, it was necessary for me to use smaller data-sets in certain of the regressions. When I had excluded countries that lacked some of the necessary data, a first data-set of 135 countries remained.

Two independent variables that intuitively seemed of particular interest were 'religiosity' and 'personal honesty'. They were derived from much smaller data-sets, described below: religiosity had 54 observations and personal honesty 32. In order to include these data-sets in my regressions using all fourteen independent variables the model had to be reduced to 27 countries.

The fourteen independent variables discussed below are grouped thus: ethics (2), social freedoms (2) and economic freedoms (10). The higher number of economic freedoms results from the availability of well-researched data-sets published annually in *The Index of Economic Freedom*, the most recent issue at the time being Miles et al. (2005).

The purpose of *The Index of Economic Freedom* is to establish a link between economic freedoms (the independent X variables) and prosperity (the dependent Y variable). The method of grading countries is described in detail in the publication. For each of ten measures a grade is given to individual countries ranging from 1 (very free) to 5 (very restricted). The scores for each country under the ten measures are averaged to give a single number from which is derived the ranking for that country in the summary table. In the 2005 edition of *The Index* Hong Kong was ranked as economically the freest country with a grade of 1.51, followed by Singapore, Luxembourg, Estonia, Ireland and New Zealand. The UK was in seventh position and the USA twelfth.

As all the variables in my regression model except one, personal honesty (see below), are index numbers rather than absolute numbers, my model does not answer questions about the absolute amount of corruption in any country calculated, say, in monetary values. Instead it sets out to answer the following key question:

- Which are the statistically significant independent variables that appear to be correlated with corruption?

As with any set of regression analyses appropriately interpreted, the purpose of the regression is not to find causality or precise relationships, but the results should give an indication of the types of factors that might help explain the existence of corruption.

Each of the fourteen independent variables is now discussed with a description of the hypothesis stating why it should be included in the analysis and the source from which the data come.

Non-economic variables
Religiosity

The world's main faiths, in alphabetical order, are Buddhism, Christianity, Hinduism, Islam and Judaism. All five faiths condemn theft. For example, under Sharia law – the law of Islam – thieves may have their right hand amputated, and this still occurs in fundamentalist Muslim communities. Though corruption and stealing are different under my definition, a more colloquial approach probably condemns corruption as akin to theft and therefore to be punished.

The hypothesis: The hypothesis is that because religious faiths condemn stealing they are likely to condemn corruption. From this it might be expected that a nation with a high adherence to one or more faiths, which I describe as religiosity, might have a low level of corruption and vice versa.

Source data: To measure religiosity I have used a *Survey of World Values* by the University of Michigan (1991 and 1997), which produced a table of the percentage of the adult population that attends their place of worship at least once a week.[1] The source does not say how the sample of 59 countries was chosen. The data derive from surveys commissioned locally in each country. There is a dominance of countries with a large number of Christians, but Nigeria,[2] Turkey, India, South Korea, China and Japan are included, having substantial majorities of non-Christians.

---

1   News and Information Services, University of Michigan, 412 Maynard, Ann Arbor, MI, News release, 10 December 1997.
2   Nigeria has 50 per cent Muslims, 40 per cent Christians and 10 per cent other religions. Source: www.indexmundi.com/nigeria/religions.html.

The measure of religiosity is attending a place of worship at least once a week. In the *Survey of World Values* Nigeria is reported as having the highest percentage of worshippers who attend at least once a week (89 per cent) and Russia the lowest (2 per cent).

Personal honesty

Virtually all societies, other than a very small number of tribal groups that share property, have a concept of personal property rights and ownership. Taking another's property without permission is a breach of property rights and is punished. It seems intuitively plausible that countries with high levels of personal honesty are likely to have low levels of theft and of corruption.

Hypothesis: The hypothesis is that countries with high personal honesty are likely to be less corrupt and vice versa.

Source data: To make an international comparison of personal honesty seems daunting but I have used a data-set from a highly imaginative survey by the *Reader's Digest* (Felten, 2001). In this, 1,130 wallets each containing US$50 were placed in public places in 113 cities spread across 32 countries in such a manner as to make them seem lost. Each wallet had identification in it so that the finder could easily return it to its owner. The experiment was to compare how many were returned. Even in affluent countries US$50 is a not a trivial sum, and in poorer countries it can be thought of as a most attractive windfall. If the finder decided to keep the wallet, no theft was entailed so the prospects of detection and punishment were zero. The finder was confronted not by law, not by risk, but only by his sense of personal honesty.

Table 7 **The ten countries that returned most wallets, 2000**

	Wallets returned	CPI ranking 2004
Norway	100%	8
Denmark	100%	3
Singapore	90%	5
New Zealand	83%	2
Finland	80%	1
Scotland	80%	na
Australia	70%	9
Japan	70%	24
South Korea	70%	47
Spain	70%	22
Average	81%	13.4

Source: Felten (2001) and CPI 2004

The ten countries that returned most wallets and the ten that returned the fewest are given in Table 7 and Table 8. All wallets were returned in Norway and Denmark and only 21 per cent were returned in Mexico. I have added the CPI ranking for comparison.

The *Reader's Digest* data are used in the regression model as data for personal honesty. Clearly, academic rigour would require examination of the way in which the wallets were deposited to ensure that bias was avoided. Further, the temptation to take US$50 is higher in poor states than in wealthy, so it would have been desirable to adjust the number of dollars in each wallet by income per head in the state concerned.

More fundamentally, the size of the sample can be criticised. It would be unwise to form strong conclusions about the relative personal honesty of nations of millions from the behaviour of as few as 120 individuals in each of the USA, Canada and Mexico and just ten individuals in other states. That said, these data have the value of being concrete, practical and available. Further, they

Table 8 **The ten countries that returned fewest wallets, 2000**

	Wallets returned	CPI ranking 2004
Belgium	50%	17
Taiwan	50%	35
Malaysia	50%	39
Germany	45%	15
Portugal	45%	27
Argentina	44%	108
Russia	43%	90
Philippines	40%	102
Italy	35%	42
Switzerland	35%	7
Hong Kong	30%	na
Mexico	21%	64
Average	41%	49.6

Source: Felten (2001) and CPI 2004

show a reasonable concordance with the results of the CPI 2004.

The average of wallets returned in the ten most honest countries was 81 per cent and those countries had an average CPI ranking of 13.4. As seen in Table 8, the average number of wallets returned in the ten least honest countries was 41 per cent, and they had an average CPI ranking of 49.6.

Freedom of the media

News frequently consists of the publication of information that someone wants to conceal. A classic example is the work of Woodward and Bernstein of the *Washington Post* in exposing the Watergate scandal that caused Richard Nixon's resignation. It seems obvious that only a free press can expose and report wrongdoing of many kinds in society.

The freedom of the media extends beyond regulations about

what the media may or may not publish with impunity. This freedom is put at risk if ownership is concentrated in few hands. Italy provides a striking example of the power and danger of permitting the wide-scale capture of the press and television by one person. Over a period of 25 years Silvio Berlusconi built a conglomerate that now dominates Italian commercial television. It has become Europe's second-largest media empire after Bertelsmann of Germany and it is Italy's third-biggest private company. This communicative power helped Berlusconi to launch a new political party and to become prime minister in just four months.[3]

Just as free media are a primary instrument to combat corruption and other forms of wrongdoing, so governments that restrict the freedom of the media have more opportunity for corruption and criminality. President Ceausescu of Romania required his name to be mentioned a given number of times on every page of every newspaper. More recently President Robert Mugabe has had the last of the independent newspapers in Zimbabwe closed down. In June 2004 the Media and Information Commission shut down Africa Tribune Newspapers, publishers of *The Tribune*, ostensibly for failing to report changes in the paper's shareholding structure.[4] It was reported that the ban would remain in force for one year. At the time of writing the BBC remains banned from reporting in Zimbabwe.

Hypothesis: The hypothesis is that the freer the media in a given jurisdiction, the lower the level of corruption.

---

3   www.museum.tv/archives/etv/B/htmlB/berlusconis/berlusconis.htm.
4   *Independent*, Harare, 11 June 2004.

Source data: A thoroughly researched annual report on press freedom worldwide is published by Freedom House, a non-partisan, US research institute founded over 50 years ago. Since 1979 it has published an annual index of the freedom of the press, currently covering 187 countries (Sussman and Guida et al., 2003).

Freedom House's method takes account of the following:

1   the structure of the news-delivery system: the laws and administrative decisions and their influence on the content of news media;
2   the degree of political influence over the content of news media;
3   economic influences on media content, including pressure on media from market competition in the private sector and related dependence on funding from political or economic interests; and
4   the intensity of repression faced by journalists in particular countries, including instances of physical attack, censorship, arrest and other harassment. Broadcast and print media are assessed separately.

The first three categories (laws, political and economic influences) are scored from 0 to 15. The lower the number, the freer the media. The fourth category (degree of violations) is scored from 0 to 5. The authors add a discretionary 0 to 5 points to a country's score to reflect the frequency and severity of violations.

The data come from overseas correspondents, staff travelling overseas, international visitors, the findings of human rights (including press freedom) organisations, specialists in geographic and geopolitical areas, the reports of governments including the US State Department, and from a variety of domestic and international news media.

Personal freedom

Could the existence or the absence of personal freedom in a given society be a cause of corruption? Intuition does not suggest a clear hypothesis. Consider the days of America's Wild West. Even allowing for its glamorisation by Hollywood, it is clear that, for a period in parts of the West, gun law ruled and that the ownership of cattle, land and the rights to prospect for gold could be ensured only by six-shooters. In such circumstances was personal freedom high or low? Citizens were free to own a gun and to use it. On the other hand personal freedom may be found more in the protection of property rights under the law than in the freedom to take the law into one's own hands.

In industrialised societies today there is continual encroachment in terms of the amount and nature of government intervention directed both at business and individuals. Governmental regulations increasingly affect health and safety, working hours and conditions, noise levels, pollution, carbon emissions, building regulations, planning approvals, recycling and a huge range of corporate activities. At an individual level increasing restrictions on smoking in public and a ban on hunting with dogs are seen by some as a reduction in civil liberties. Others see restrictions on smoking as an increase in the civil liberties of non-smokers not to inhale others' smoke. A particularly topical issue in the UK is whether compulsory ID cards would reduce civil liberties or increase them by making certain crimes harder to get away with, for example social security fraud, illegal immigration and illegal employment.

Hypothesis: The hypothesis is that corruption is lower in countries in which political rights and civil liberties are high.

Source data: Freedom House publishes two indices in this connection: one for political rights and another for civil liberties. In both indices the freest countries are graded 1 and the least free are graded 7.

The survey rates the rights and freedoms enjoyed by individuals as the result of actions by both state and non-governmental actors. The methodology uses standards drawn from the Universal Declaration of Human Rights which are applied to all states and territories, irrespective of geographical location, ethnic or religious composition or level of economic development. The survey does not base its judgement solely on the political conditions in a country or territory (e.g., war, terrorism), but on the effect that these conditions have on freedom.[5]

I suggest that there is an obvious overlap between political rights and civil liberties. The right to form a political party, the right to vote, the right to strike and the right to demonstrate might equally be termed political rights or civil liberties. In Freedom House's two data series the two gradings for a given country are predominantly the same number. In regression analysis if data for two sets of independent variables are almost the same results

---

5   Freedom House, *Freedom in the World 2003: Survey Methodology*, www.freedomhouse.org/template.cfm?page=15&year=2005.

·of the regression are likely to be unreliable because the sets give rise to auto-correlation. To avoid this, I merged the two indices, taking an average between the two numbers for countries when they varied, which was seldom.

Ten economic freedoms

The Heritage Foundation, Washington, DC, and the *Wall Street Journal* produce an annual *Index of Economic Freedom*.[6] The 2005 edition covers 150 countries. Every country is scored under ten indices, each of which represents an aspect of economic freedom: 1.0 is the highest mark (most free) and 5.0 is the lowest (least free). The average score for each country gives its overall index, from which an international ranking is produced. The data are then illustrated on a graph with per-head income as the dependent Y variable and the combined economic freedom index as the independent X variable. The graph shows a steadily rising curve by which the countries with the lowest economic freedoms have the lowest per capita incomes and vice versa.[7]

The *Index of Economic Freedom* data offer the possibility of examining whether there is a relationship between the level of economic freedom as the independent variable and the level of perceived corruption (the CPI) as the dependent.

Following the index's numbering system, I now set out hypotheses about why each of the index's ten economic freedoms might drive or be correlated with the level of corruption in each country.

---

6   Miles et al. (2005); the Institute of Economic Affairs is the UK partner organisa-
     tion for the index.

7   Ibid., p. 18.

Trade policy (1)

Governments can impose barriers to trade, mainly through import tariffs but also through quotas. The latter can be a particularly fruitful source of corruption. Officials who allocate quotas know that if quotas are required to restrict imports, the price that importers are willing to pay in addition to import duties is higher than the price set by foreign suppliers. Therefore, to obtain some part of the quota importers must be willing to pay bribes to functionaries allocating the quota if these are corrupt.

Hypothesis: The hypothesis is that the more trade restrictions a country has the higher its level of corruption.

Data source: Miles et al., 2005

Fiscal burden of government (2)

All governments need to levy taxes in order to finance goods and services that are genuinely 'public goods' (such as defence) or whose provision has been allocated to the public sector through the democratic process. Many activities undertaken by government that do not need to be financed from the public purse are, however, paid for from taxation: education and health, for example. In general, the larger the share of government expenditure in national income, the higher the rates of direct and indirect taxation needed to pay for the government's consumption. The higher the overall level of taxation, the higher the incentive to avoid or evade paying tax.[8] This could lead to corruption. For

---

8   The grey area between tax *avoidance* (legal) and tax *evasion* (illegal) was dubbed tax *avoision* by the late Arthur Seldon, the IEA's first editorial director.

example, a tax inspector might be bribed to reduce a tax demand or an accountant could be bribed to present false accounts.

Hypothesis: The hypothesis is that corruption is higher in countries with higher fiscal burdens.

Data source for fiscal burdens: Miles et al., 2005

Government intervention in the economy (3)

The Index of Economic Freedom states: 'This factor measures government's direct use of scarce resources for it own purposes and government's control over resources through ownership' (ibid.: 65). It does not intuitively follow that if a functionary instead of a private sector manager runs, say, an airline, there will be more corruption unless the functionary is paid less than a market wage for doing so. The functionary may then seek to increase his earnings to a market wage or higher by taking bribes for allocating the contracts that every airline awards, such as that for the provision of in-flight meals.

Hypothesis: The hypothesis is that the higher the level of government intervention in the economy, the higher the level of corruption.

Data source for the level of government intervention: Miles et al., 2005

Monetary policy (4)

The value of a country's currency in most cases is determined by decisions made by the government, though some developed countries have now given their central banks independence in setting interest rates to control inflation and hence to provide the currency with stability. Delinquent governments that print money and pursue inflationary policies may contain corrupt politicians who put money into Swiss bank accounts. Also, where a government does not pursue a transparent monetary and/or exchange rate policy, there is often high inflation. This in turn provides opportunities for the selling of inside information, for example on the timing of the change of exchange rate parities.

Hypothesis: The hypothesis is that countries with weak monetary policies are more likely to be corrupt.

Data source for the strength/weakness of monetary policy: Miles et al., 2005

Capital flows and foreign investment (5)

Restrictions on foreign investment limit the inflow and outflow of capital and may be matched by restrictions on the repatriation of dividends. As with the authorisation of quotas for imports, those who control the movements of funds are in a position to be bribed.

Hypothesis: The hypothesis is that those countries with restrictions on the movement of funds are more likely to be corrupt than those with few or no restrictions.

Data source for capital flows and foreign investment: Miles et al., 2005

Banking and finance (6)

Banks are facilitators. New businesses and established firms need credit, individuals need loans to buy homes and consumer durables, and they all need safe places in which to store their money. *The Index of Economic Freedom* states that: 'The more banks are controlled by the government, the less free they are to engage in these activities' (ibid.: 70).

Some regulation of the banking sector seems desirable because if banks become insolvent there can be serious economic disruption and loss of confidence. Firms and individuals lose their assets, payments systems can break down and the aftermath may take a long time to clear up. The collapse of the Bank of Credit and Commerce International (BCCI) in 1991 is an example that persisted until November 2005, when the bank's creditors finally dropped their lawsuit against the Bank of England.

In the case of BCCI, Enron, Worldcom and other recent high-profile corporate failures it seems that there was more theft than corruption. These issues were discussed fully in Chapter 2.

Nevertheless, it does not seem to be strongly intuitive that the regulation of banking and financial systems will prove to be a significant cause of corruption. On the one hand, if strong regulation of the banking sector prevents fraud, corruption may fall. On the other hand, regulation may make the financial system more complex and increase the opportunities for the corruption of public officials, so the opposite also seems possible. Even so, since data are available I have added the banking and finance index to the independent variables.

Hypothesis: The hypothesis is that states with highly regulated banking and financing systems are likely to be more corrupt than those with greater freedom.

Data source for intervention in banking and finance: Miles et al., 2005

Wages and prices (7)

In a market economy prices are signals that enable resources to be allocated their use of highest value. In western Europe the central-ised control of certain prices still occurs in limited contexts. The most common of these, paradoxically, is when a market is liber-alised. For example, former state monopolists that are privatised at least initially have a highly dominant share of the market and in these circumstances some safeguards are used to prevent them from making profits from dominance rather than from efficiency in the market. In the UK a common form of price control has been based on movement in the retail price index less a percentage determined in some way. The system is known as 'RPI-X'. Once a transparent and competitive market has been established there is no case for price control.

Direct governmental regulation of wage rates is fairly uncommon in western Europe but it remains the Holy Grail of trade unions, which continue to believe in a 'rate for the job' in the form of a standard wage package across the country for their members. Though such packages may stave off industrial action, they produce their own problems. A nationwide package typically fails to attract enough labour in the some parts of the country while being over-generous in others.

One form of governmental intervention in the UK is a national minimum wage. This was introduced by the Labour government in 1998 and has been increased periodically since then. Another way by which a government can influence the cost of labour in the market is by regulating working hours. Such regulation may affect, for example, the hours of lorry drivers. In France, on the other hand, a blanket 35-hour working week was introduced in 1998 in an attempt to tackle high unemployment. The government hoped that firms would have to take on more staff to maintain a given level of output. The policy has failed and France's unemployment rate remains currently at about 10 per cent compared with less than 3 per cent in the UK. Both Jean-Pierre Raffarin and Dominique de Villepin, two of France's recent revolving-door prime ministers, have attempted to mitigate the law in question, bringing widespread demonstrations on to the streets.

Government intervention on prices is known to cause secondary markets for goods to emerge in command economies. This was exemplified in the Soviet Union, despite fearsome penalties on those who operated them. It is less obvious that intervention in labour markets causes corruption to develop, though it certainly encourages cheating. For example, illegal immigrants were hired for cockle-picking in Morecambe Bay. This was not corrupt, though it arguably gave rise to a serious accident when many were drowned.[9]

Hypothesis: The hypothesis is that where governments intervene

9   For a discussion of the many complex issues raised by the Morecambe Bay tragedy, see Meadowcroft and Blundell (2004).

on prices and in labour markets there will be higher levels of corruption.

Data source for government intervention in wages and prices: Miles et al., 2005

Property rights regulation (8)

The ownership of goods, land and buildings is a fundamental form of property rights. The ownership of intellectual property rights is also essential because without them there is no incentive to invent, test and market a new product if it can be copied with impunity. Copying is not corrupt, though it may be commercially wrong and illegal as well, depending on the prevailing laws.

Hypothesis: The hypothesis is that countries with weak property rights have correspondingly higher levels of corruption.

Data source for property rights: Miles et al., 2005

Regulation (9)

It seems clear that some regulation is desirable in an economy, at least to deal with harmful effects on third parties. Very liberal economists put their faith in the courts, envisaging that wronged third parties can seek legal redress, rather than in specific regulation. But it seems unsatisfactory that, say, a group of individuals should first have to wait for a factory to belch toxic fumes, to suffer for a period and then to have to prove and evaluate their suffering in a law court, but only when the effect of their suffering becomes measurable. Government regulation seems a more effective way of dealing with such problems in the first place.

Finding the right level of regulation is not easy, and the present trend within the EU is for more and more specific – some would say irksome – regulation. The theory is that the single market will work better if all producers are subject to the same regulations. It seems likely, however, that if regulations are disproportionately intrusive, businesses and individuals will seek ways to avoid the cost that compliance entails. Are higher levels of regulation likely to be correlated with higher levels of corruption?

The extent of regulation faced by a start-up business in the UK is given below. In *The Index of Economic Freedom*, 2005, the UK scores 2 for the extent of its regulation (1 being little regulated and 5 being highly regulated). If the UK scores quite well on this measure, countries with higher scores must have regulations that are even more daunting in volume and complexity.

The following print-out from a DTI Internet checklist (see Box 1) represents the *areas* of regulation (not the regulations themselves) that affect a manufacturing firm that also directly markets its services. The list is reproduced verbatim. For each of the headings and subheadings on the website a click takes you to further detail, possibly of several pages. Each of these pages has headings and links to yet more pages, and so on. Readers do not have to read the checklist that follows, let alone the sub-checklists or the sub-sub-checklists that are accessed from the website. I keep the list in the main body of the text, however, rather than exile it to an appendix, as most appendices go unread. Lay people reading this book should be encouraged to experience the *pain* that regulation emanating from functionaries in Brussels and the UK inflicts on producers of goods and services demanded by the market.

It is possible that if regulation reaches too high a level, corruption will follow. For example, factories will see potential gains from bribing inspectors. As some of the regulations might well be pointless, adverse consequences are unlikely to arise and the bribery is likely not to be discovered. On the other hand, it is interesting to note that Chile, Switzerland, Sweden, the Netherlands, Germany and Austria all score 3 in *The Index of Economic Freedom* for the prevalence of regulation (meaning that they have high regulation) and yet feature in the top twenty of the CPI 2004 (meaning that they are at the uncorrupt end of the index).

Hypothesis: Although intuition does not automatically suggest a hypothesis in relation to the level of regulation in a jurisdiction, the one that I have made is that the heavier the burden of regulation, the higher the level of corruption. This is based on the assumption that those who are regulated may bribe regulators in order to get round irksome regulations.

Data source for the level of regulation: Miles et al., 2005

Informal markets (10)

Views among economists and others vary as to whether informal markets – variously described as secondary, grey or black – are benign, malign or neutral in an economy. In Chapter 5 of *The Index of Economic Freedom*, 2005, Beach and Miles (2005) group the following as 'informal market activities':

1   smuggling;
2   piracy of intellectual property in the informal market;

Box 1 THE DTI'S REGULATION CHECKLIST*

Step 5: Your regulation checklist
Below is a checklist of guides on our site about regulations likely to affect your business.

Each guide links to a plain English explanation. Remember – the list may not be definitive, but it is a simple, flexible tool to help you find out what you need to do.

What would you like to do with your checklist?
• Save my answers so I can read the guides at my own pace
• Email my checklist to me (and save my answers)
• Email me when my guides are updated (and save my answers)

We recommend that you choose one of the options above in order to keep your checklist for future use.

Here is your regulation checklist
Starting up
Financial control, operations and transport
• Assess your business transport requirements
• Operating your own motor vehicles

Taxes, returns & payroll
Introduction to business taxes
• Accounting and audit exemptions for small companies

VAT
• VAT: the basics

*www.businesslink.gov.uk/bdotg/action/prglGuideList.

- How much VAT should you charge?
- Change your VAT registration
- Cancel your VAT registration

National Insurance
- National Insurance contributions for self-employed people
- National Insurance contributions for employers
- Pay National Insurance contributions for directors

PAYE and payroll
- Operate a year-round PAYE system
- Sort out your PAYE affairs for the end of the tax year
- Manage tax credits
- Manage student loans, payroll and other deductions
- Taxable benefits

Corporation tax
- Corporation tax: the basics
- Make corporation tax payments

Income tax
- Income tax self assessment: the basics
- Income tax rates and allowances
- Income tax self assessment for directors

Business expenses
- Business expenses and dispensations
- Company cars, vans and fuel

Business rates and other taxes
- Stamp duty: the basics

- Taxes for specific products, services and activities

Tax help and inspections
- Penalties, late payments and late returns

Choosing and setting up a legal structure
- Change your business structure

Administration, records and reporting
- Balance sheets: the basics
- Company administration: the basics
- Company directors' responsibilities
- Company secretaries' responsibilities
- Companies House annual return (form 363)
- File accounts at Companies House
- Change your accounting date
- Shares and shareholders

Online tax and filing services
- Key filing dates

Employing people
Recruitment and getting started
- Employing part-timers
- Using contractors and subcontractors

Paperwork
- The employment contract
- Keep the right staff records

Paying your staff
- Pay – an overview of obligations
- PAYE: the basics
- National Insurance: the basics

Pension schemes
- Know your legal obligations on pensions

Setting the rules
- Monitoring and security of staff

Working time and time off
- Maternity, paternity and adoption – an overview

Equal opportunities
- Prevent discrimination and value diversity

Motivation
- Inform and consult your employees

Dismissals, redundancies and other exits
- Workers leaving: the basics
- Dismissal

Disciplinary problems, disputes and grievances
- Handling discipline and grievance issues
- Bullying and harassment
- Reduce the risk of employment tribunal claims
- Industrial disputes

Health, safety, premises
Managing health, safety & environment
- Importance of health, safety & environment to your business
- Your responsibilities for health, safety and the environment
- Create and implement a health, safety and environment policy
- Risk assessment – an overview
- Communicate your health and safety procedures
- Register for health and safety
- Record and report an accident, incident or near miss

Working environment
- Meet minimum workplace standards
- Facilities for customers and employees
- Smoking policies, drugs and alcohol abuse
- Pollution, effluent and the management of waste
- Disposal of old equipment: your responsibilities

Working practices
- Food safety
- Protect yourself
- Ensure employees' safety when lifting and carrying
- Ensure the safe use of machinery, equipment and tools
- Transport in the workplace
- Transporting goods and materials
- Storing goods and materials

People, health and welfare
- Occupational health and welfare: an overview
- Hours, rest breaks and the working week
- Employing young people

- Prevent RSI and other upper-limb disorders
- First aid
- How to deal with stress
- Diseases, infections and allergies

Premises
- Buying or renting business premises
- Responsibilities of landlords and tenants
- Planning permission and building regulations
- Access and facilities for disabled people
- Fire safety and risk assessment

Help, finance and advisers
- Business rates
- Environmental tax obligations and breaks

Exploit your ideas
Protecting your intellectual property
- Intellectual property: the basics

IT & e-commerce
Staff and IT
- Ensure your employees are operating computers safely

Data protection, privacy & security
- Data privacy

Sales and marketing
Marketing
- Direct marketing: the basics

Pricing
- Price fixing, cartels, monopolies & the new Enterprise Act

Selling and the law
- Product liability
- Weights and measures
- Product labelling and packaging
- Comply with advertising standards
- Ensure your products are safe

International trade
International trade basics
- Importing – an overview
- Exporting – an overview
- Do I need an export licence?

International trade finance
- Trading in the European Union
- Insurance for international trade

Tax and paperwork
- VAT on sales to EC countries
- Complete the Intrastat return

Logistics and distribution
- Handling logistics and paperwork – importing and exporting
- Shipping

Improve your business
Best practice and standards
- Make best use of standards

Identify and manage risks
- Liability insurance

Buy or sell a business
Buying a business
- Growing your business: mergers and acquisitions

In your sector
Manufacturing & engineering
- Regulation – manufacturing and engineering

We can offer further help with regulations:
Find out what licences and permits you need to operate your business
Use our licence tool to find out which licences and permits could apply to your business

Order the free No-Nonsense Guide to Regulations
If you're thinking of running a business or working for yourself, the 100-page No-Nonsense Guide tells you what you need to know about the legal and official side of starting up on your own.

What would you like to do with your checklist?
Save my answers so I can read the guides at my own pace
Email my checklist to me (and save my answers)
Email me when my guides are updated (and save my answers)

We recommend that you choose one of the options above in order to **keep your checklist** for future use.

3 agricultural production supplied on the informal market;
4 manufacturing supplied on the informal market;
5 services supplied on the informal market;
6 transportation supplied on the informal market;
7 labour supplied on the informal market.

Many readers might be against Item 2, piracy of intellectual property, but turned a blind eye when their children were down-loading music and films free from pirate websites. Attitudes towards Item 1, smuggling, are also equivocal. A substantial proportion of cigarettes sold in the UK are known to have been smuggled into the country and many smokers have no inhibitions about buying cheap cigarettes with no questions asked.

Items 3 and 4 seem positively benign if farmers' markets and car boot sales are included, providing that the goods in the latter have not been stolen and are not counterfeit.

Items 5 and 7 – services and labour supplied on the informal market – require elucidation. If the services are supplied by illegal immigrants who are exploited by gang-masters for a pittance, as in the case of the Morecambe Bay cockle-pickers mentioned earlier, we would probably agree that this is undesirable, though of course the solution is to prevent illegal immigration in the first place.[10] If informal services entail the avoidance of income tax and VAT through cash transactions, law-abiding citizens might agree that cheating the Revenue is undesirable because the remainder who don't cheat must pay more tax collectively for a given tax yield. Even so, many law-abiding citizens have no qualms about paying the plumber in cash.

---

10   Again, see Meadowcroft and Blundell (2004).

Item 6 – transport supplied on the informal market – is likely to be considered undesirable. Taxi meters, if they have not been doctored, give passengers, particularly foreigners, some protection against being cheated. Further, a licensed cab plying for trade is subject to more stringent safety checks than an ordinary car. Similar protection may, however, be provided through certification rather than licensing, with non-certified cabs being excluded.

In essence, the bundle of attributes of informal markets that are used in *The Index of Economic Freedom* do not all seem necessarily to be associated with corruption, though it may be the case that they are more likely to occur in corrupt economies. The case of communist Russia, discussed earlier, illustrates how informal markets develop because ordinary market forces have been suppressed. Nearer to home, the rules imposed by the All England Lawn Tennis and Croquet Club prohibiting the resale of tickets for the Wimbledon tennis championships show how an informal market immediately comes into being when regulation eliminates the forces of supply and demand for popular events that cannot even remotely be thought of as the necessities of life.

Hypothesis: The hypothesis is that informal markets are more likely to develop in regimes where corruption is high.

Data source for the extent of informal markets: Miles et al., 2005

Normalising the data

All the data-sets except for personal honesty (wallets returned) derive either from percentages such as church attenders (religiosity) or from indices. The original data had indices from 0 to 10,

Figure 1 Testing the causes of corruption, 2005

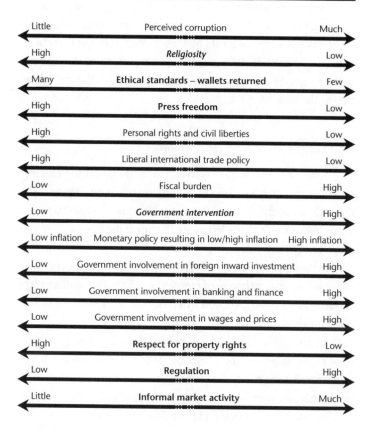

Note: The drivers that proved statistically significant are in **bold**. Those in ***bold italics*** were negatively significant. See text.

Figure: Ian Senior

1 to 7 and 1 to 5. I therefore transformed all the index numbers to lie between 0 and 10 so that the values of the X parameters in each regression would be comparable with each other. This would serve to show which of the Xs had most effect upon (or correlation with) the independent Y variable. I then transformed the data-sets in the expectation of making the variables move in the same direction as the stated hypotheses.

Summary of the independent variables

The dependent variable, perceived corruption, and the fourteen independent variables are shown schematically in Figure 1. The dependent variable Y (the Corruption Perceptions Index) is shown at the top. A move to the left along the line indicates a *reduction* in perceived corruption.

The hypothesis is that perceived corruption is the dependent variable and that a change of any of the drivers (the independent variables) in a given direction will move the level of corruption in the same direction.

The X variables in bold are those that proved statistically significant in the regression tests described below. Those that are in *bold italics* proved negatively significant, that is to say they produced a result that ran counter to my intuitive hypotheses. These results are discussed in more detail in the following chapter.

4 THE REGRESSION MODEL'S RESULTS

As described earlier, my regression model uses data from referenced sources to identify statistically significant correlations with perceived corruption. Various combinations of the independent variables were used, as described below. The smaller number of observations for some regression tests resulted from smaller datasets in the source data.

I do not intend to embark on a discussion of whether a statistically significant correlation between the Y variable and any of the X variables shows *causation.* It is possible that they are both influenced by some other variable that has not been included in the model. The direction of causation between the Y variable and any of the Xs cannot be determined by regression analysis. For example, it could reasonably be argued that if corruption in a jurisdiction increases, this *causes* property rights to diminish; or that corruption in a highly regulated market *causes* an informal market to develop.

Nevertheless, a likely direction of causation is given in my hypotheses, and when the model finds X variables that are positive and statistically significant these become prime candidates for being the *likely determinants* of corruption. It is worth restating here that I am looking for patterns in data that should help us understand the phenomenon of corruption: prediction is not my aim.

Test 1: fourteen independent variables

The first regression used all fourteen independent variables. The data-set covered 27 countries, namely those for which there were observations for every variable. With fourteen variables and only 27 observations it was likely that statistically significant independent variables would be scant. The t-test showed significance only for 'informal markets', whose sign was positive as predicted by the hypothesis. In other words, corruption is more likely to be high in countries where informal markets abound. This accords with the widely observed fact that informal markets occur when state regulation stifles the working of markets generally.

Test 2: twelve independent variables

The independent variables 'religiosity' and 'wallets returned' were those with fewest observations. Some countries had no observations in either set. For the second test these two variables were therefore excluded, giving observations for 135 countries. The t-test showed statistical significance for 'government intervention in the economy', 'property rights', 'regulation' and 'informal markets'.

In the case of the last three of these, the sign of the relationship was positive, namely as expected by the hypothesis. In the case of government intervention, however – meaning a government's direct use of scarce resources for its own purposes and government control over resources through ownership – the negative sign of the t-statistic means that according to the model higher government intervention drives or is correlated with lower corruption. This result is counter-intuitive and would merit further research.

Two points are worth noting at this stage. First, it is possible that many of the independent variables are strongly correlated (for example, government intervention and government involvement in foreign inward investment). This could lead to statistically significant correlations not being picked up in this analysis, although it is not clear how this should lead to a negative correlation between government intervention and corruption. It is also worth noting that there are some significant countries, such as the Scandinavian economies, in which the government's share of GDP is high and in which there are low levels of corruption. It would be very difficult to argue that a high level of government intervention causes 'uncorruption' in these countries.

Test 3: four independent variables

In Test 3 I excluded all ten economic freedom variables, leaving the first four variables: religiosity, wallets returned, press freedom and personal freedom. There were observations for 27 countries. The t-statistic showed significance for religiosity and press freedom. The t-statistic for press freedom was positive, meaning that the more press freedom there is, the less corruption, which is intuitively satisfactory.

The t-statistic for religiosity, however, was negative, implying that higher religiosity in the form of attendance at worship once or more per week is associated with more corruption. This was intuitively unexpected, and personally I find it disappointing that religiosity apparently does not provide a bulwark against corruption. But nor does it provide a bulwark against violence and terrorism, as witnessed in Northern Ireland for 30 years, along with the former Yugoslavia, Iraq and other countries of the Middle East, where religiosity succeeds in separating sections of the community and justifies their violence against each other.

In 22 of the 27 countries the population attending church is predominantly Christian of various denominations: Catholic, Protestant and Orthodox. It is disheartening that high overt religiosity, far from repressing corruption, seems to make it more common.

Test 4: one independent variable – wallets returned

An intuitively attractive hypothesis is that a nation's personal honesty developed over generations may be stronger than many other independent variables. My fourth test regressed the data for returned wallets against the CPI data for the 32 countries of the *Reader's Digest* survey. The coefficient of correlation (R^2) was 0.32 and the t-statistic was significant at 3.81. This result supports a view that the importance of individuals' inbred personal honesty may strongly determine the amount of corruption prevailing in a jurisdiction as a whole. After all, uncorruption is simply another aspect of honesty.

Test 5: corruption and GDP per head

I tested a fifth hypothesis: is there a relationship between corruption and GDP per head? Casual observation leads to interesting results. For example, prosperous Singapore is ranked fifth in the CPI 2004 but there is much lower prosperity and higher corruption in its much larger neighbours Malaysia (=39 in the CPI 2004), Thailand (= 64), the Philippines (=102) and Indonesia (=133).

For the reasons discussed in the following chapter, corruption may restrain the growth of GDP and hence of GDP per head because there is less inward investment and the cost of capital is

Figure 2   **Relationship between perceived corruption and GDP per head, 2005**

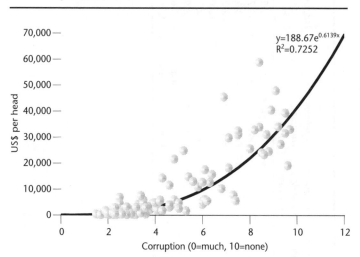

Figure: Ian Senior

higher. Case studies show that corrupt economies are prone to inefficiency. My hypothesis therefore was that GDP per head is the dependent variable and the CPI 2004 as a proxy for corruption is an independent variable. In essence, the more corrupt a country, the lower its GDP per head is likely to be. The data-set was 134 countries, with GDP per head for 2002, using constant US dollars for 1995 (Miles et al., 2005).

The results are shown in Figure 2. The coefficient of correlation, R^2, was 0.73, showing that a considerable correlation exists, and the t-statistic was strongly significant at 18.9.

From the figure it can be seen that there is a large and dense group of countries at the lowest part of the curve, with GDP

Table 9 Summary of regression results

Independent variables tested

	Names	Number	Observations number	Significant variables, number	Significant variables, names	T-statistic
Test 1	All	14	27	1	Informal market	5.8
Test 2	All excluding religiosity and wallets returned	12	135	4	Govt intervention	-2.7
					Property rights	3.2
					Regulation	2.2
					Informal market	13.0
Test 3	Religiosity, wallets returned, press freedom, personal freedom	4	27	2	Religiosity	-2.2
					Press freedom	2.9
Test 4	Wallets returned	1	32	1	Wallets returned	3.6
Test 5	Perceived Corruption Index	1	134	1	Perceived corruption	18.9

Table: Ian Senior

per head below US$5,000, which have high perceived corruption ratings. From a perceived corruption rating of about 5 and upwards, as corruption diminishes, both the slope of the curve and GDP per head increase steadily. The hypothesis that corruption serves to constrain GDP per head is supported by Figure 2.

Summary of the five regression tests

The t-statistics from the five tests are shown in Table 9. Seven of the fourteen independent variables proved statistically significant though two of them — government intervention and religiosity — produced a negative t-statistic, meaning that the results were counter-intuitive. I am not much concerned about whether religiosity is considered as being associated with corruption or simply coexisting with it.

The positive correlation between government intervention and uncorruption seems intuitively plausible only if the government itself is uncorrupt. Further research might throw light on this question. It should be noted that regressions of this sort are a fairly blunt instrument that may leave uncovered nuances in the relationships. For example, if several variables are themselves correlated or if corruption is correlated with a particular form of intervention, or with a high level of intervention only in poor countries, then these features may not be found from regression.

5   CONSEQUENCES OF CORRUPTION

I contend that the following are the consequences of corruption in any country and at any time:

- price distortion occurs even when markets appear to clear;
- a covert, upward redistribution of wealth takes place within society;
- democratic processes are subverted;
- financial and commercial risks that affect the willingness to invest are increased; and
- society's morality and ethics decline.

I now provide examples of empirical studies that support these five contentions.

Price distortion even when markets appear to clear

When bribes are needed to gain contracts the price paid by the winning contractor exceeds the value of the work that would be done in an uncorrupt market. The balance is paid to the corruptee or retained as excess profit by the corruptor. If an asset has been created through a corruptly awarded contract, a higher return is needed. For example, the higher cost of a toll bridge built by a corruptor who had to pay a bribe requires a higher toll to produce a given rate of return. Thus, the users of the bridge pay for the bribe. If the bridge has no tolls and so provides no monetary return, the additional cost is borne by the treasury and, in turn, by taxpayers.

Estimates have been made to quantify the excessive costs of corruptly tendered contracts in Italy in the 1980s and early 1990s. In June 1993, at the time of the Clean Hands investigation in Milan, bribes on telecommunications contracts were estimated at 2 per cent of the total value and on power stations at 3 per cent, but the actual costs of the projects were thought to be between 14 and 20 per cent more than was necessary. In other words, bribes not only represented an additional cost even if the chosen contractors were efficient, but they enabled contractors to inflate their prices with impunity. One estimate for the total cost of corruption in Italy was $5 billion (£2.75 billion) a year. Although many bribes were supposed to be contributions to political parties, those who confessed to taking bribes conceded that as much as 60 per cent of the money collected ended up in the bank accounts of individuals.

The Italian chapter of Transparency International confirmed in November 1999 that after the Clean Hands operation the cost of public investments in Milan fell dramatically. The average cost per kilometre of constructing an underground railway dropped by 57 per cent and a new international airport was completed at a cost of 59 per cent less than had been estimated. The operation of municipal companies had been turned from loss to profit and municipal tax was less than in other comparable towns.[1]

---

1   UNDP PARAGON Generic Training Module, op. cit.

Covert and upward redistribution of wealth within society

Drawing on the Italian case above, if we accept that Italian politicians and functionaries were receiving $5 billion (£2.75 billion) a year in bribes and that 60 per cent of the bribes remained with the corruptees, $3 billion (£1.65 billion) would have been spent on personal assets such as houses and consumer goods or else would have been banked in Switzerland or elsewhere. More public funds would have been needed from indirect taxation, notably VAT, assuming that the capacity to levy direct taxes is more or less saturated in Italy. A general tax on all citizens is necessary to finance the excess costs of public programmes, the beneficiaries of which are generally well off.

Corrupt contracts result in expenditures that distort and diminish the benefits the public can expect to obtain from public expenditure on services such as roads, schools and hospitals. In addition, the democratic process itself is distorted by making funds available to the party in power, which in turn increases its prospects of re-election.

Other side effects are probable. When contractors (the corruptors) are compelled to bid higher prices that include bribes, they are more likely to cut corners on workmanship and to disregard safety regulations.

Kenya ranks 129th out of 146 in the CPI 2004. The upward redistribution of money from corruption in Kenya has been quantified to some degree. In 2002 Transparency International (TI) launched a study called the Kenya Urban Bribery Index, based on a survey of 1,164 individuals from several Kenyan towns. Mati and Mwangi (2003) found as follows.

- The average urban Kenyan paid eighteen bribes a month, amounting to $104 (£93) per month compared with an average monthly income among the survey respondents of $331 (£295). This means that there is a redistribution of income of 31 per cent from those at the bottom of society's pyramid who have no positions of authority from which they can collect bribes to offset those they have paid.
- Public servants were bribed the most, accounting for 99 per cent of all bribery transactions and 97 per cent of the total value of bribes given.
- Other bribes were made to the private sector and foreign organisations such as embassies and international agencies.
- The police were the worst offenders for taking bribes. Six out of ten urban residents reported paying bribes to the police, observing that failure to do so led to mistreatment or the denial of service.
- The next-worst offenders were the Ministry of Public Works followed by the immigration department.

When TI's report and index were published, predictable denials from many of the named ministries and organisations ensued, though a few admitted that the report was accurate. The deputy mayor of Nairobi City Council agreed that his institution was among the most corrupt in Kenya. For two weeks after the report was published the police stopped demanding bribes at roadblocks.

Romania ranks =87th in the CPI 2004. An extremely high level of corruption exists in its health services. In 2005 a study financed by the World Bank showed that Romanians pay approximately

US$1 million (£570,000) a day in bribes to medical staff.[2] The bribes are paid by patients to doctors and nurses because they feel the need to hand over cash to guarantee a basic standard of service. In the study one in ten patients said that nurses suggested or had told them directly that they would need to pay them for treatment, and one in 20 patients said that doctors had told them the same. Though most Romanians believed that offering money to medical staff is a form of bribery, one in five said they had willingly agreed to the payments.

The health sectors of eastern European countries are described by those within the systems as a hangover from the former communist regimes, where low-level corruption was rife yet tacitly accepted in all levels of society. As noted earlier, however, in Greece a *fakelaki* is a cash 'gift' for the doctor before an operation or medical treatment which is thought to guarantee the best possible care for a patient and a nicer room at public hospitals. Greece is not a former communist state although it has had left-wing governments.

Whether bribes are paid willingly or not, they represent a covert and illegal tax on people when they need treatment and operations and are least able to refuse. In Romania doctors and nurses are thought to be badly paid even by local standards, and this may salve their consciences in soliciting and receiving bribes. The World Bank's study does not determine whether the bribes are effective in actually increasing the standard of medical care supplied by the staff who have been bribed. What is certain is that the bribes represent a form of protection money or extortion and are paid by patients who fear the consequences if they don't give bribes.

2   C. Ionescu, *The Lancet*, 29 October 2005.

The three exemplar countries, Italy, Kenya and Romania, show how in industrialised, ex-communist and underdeveloped countries alike, when corruption takes hold there is a significant distortion of individual incomes. When bribes are paid by individuals this transfer is generally from the lower-paid members of society upwards. When they are paid by corporations they go to politicians who are already reasonably paid by local standards. If they are spent on luxury imports or deposited in Swiss bank accounts they have no trickle-down effect.

It is the hallmark of sub-Saharan African governments that when presidents retire or are ousted, they are very rich indeed. For example, since General Sani Abacha, president of Nigeria, died in 1998 investigators have so far recovered about $1 billion (£540 million) from bank accounts in Switzerland, Jersey, Liechtenstein and Luxembourg. General Abacha combined accepting massive bribes with siphoning money directly from the Nigerian treasury, which is kleptocracy, not corruption. As noted earlier, one estimate is that he amassed about $3 billion (£1.6 billion) in five years.[3]

Democratic processes are subverted

From France, Germany and Italy in the West to Japan in the East, and in many countries in between, bribes paid to ministers and politicians have been used to finance political parties. On paper, democratic countries pay lip-service to the concept that donations to politicians and their parties should be transparent and capped by law to prevent democracy becoming simply an expression of

---

3   *The Times*, 17 February 2005.

what those with the deepest pockets want their governments to do.

Other side effects occur, however, notably that the democratic process is overtly flouted. This is seen in the exploitation of national assets such as oil, gas, minerals or timber. Companies that spend money finding and extracting these raw materials should be rewarded for their costs and for the risks entailed, but it might be expected that the balance of their proceeds generally accrue to the nation that owns the assets.[4] In corrupt states it is clear that this does not happen.

In 1994, in an effort to reverse its poor forest management record, Cameroon's government passed a law regulating logging concessions. Despite this, a Cameroonian NGO estimated that illegal timber accounted for 45 per cent of the country's total timber production in 2000. Further, even valid concessions were being awarded under dubious circumstances. In 1998 the World Bank reported that these were awarded to the highest bidder in only ten out of 25 cases. Global Witness, an independent organisation, reported that permission to log in Cameroon invariably requires the payment of bribes.[5]

There is a difference between ignoring the law because it is not enforced on the one hand, and bribing the authorities to obtain legitimate logging concessions on the other. In Cameroon's case the two overlap. Ignoring the law is overt and should be the easier

---

4   Of course, precisely how property rights in such raw materials develop will vary from country to country: they may be wholly private. It is a matter of fact, however, that, in most states, the government has a role, rightly or wrongly, in allocating property rights (selling licences to drill oil and so on). If these licences are sold or the gains from extracting the raw material are taxed, it should be taxpayers in general who benefit. In a corrupt society this is not the case.

5   Transparency International, *Global Corruption Report*, 2003, p. 230.

to eradicate. Timber companies either have a valid licence to log in a given location or they do not. If they have no licence and the judiciary has the means to enforce the law, illegal logging ceases. But corruption, being covert, can make it seem that the law is being applied because a licence has been (corruptly) obtained. Thus corruption covertly destroys not only rainforests but democracy too. Evidence suggests that this problem prevails in many other countries that have significant rainforests.

Increased cost and reduction of investment

If you have to choose between two countries in which to make an investment to achieve a return of 5 per cent and the choice is between Finland and Haiti, where would you invest? Even without consulting the CPI you would instinctively require a much higher return from Haiti to compensate for the much higher risk of your dividend being frozen or being paid in depreciating currency or not being paid at all. But if you had to choose between a return of 5 per cent in Finland and 25 per cent in Haiti, you might be tempted to try Haiti, considering the risk premium available from Haiti as fair compensation. Haiti must offer a much higher return; and individuals or institutions will probably be willing to risk less money. Clearly when determining the amount of an investment they may make, investors take factors other than the level of corruption into account. Corruption, however, must be a significant factor that affects the value of the investment made and the interest required to justify the investment at all.

Evidence is found in Serven (1998), who regressed the volatility of five key macroeconomic variables – inflation, growth, the terms of trade, the real exchange rate and the price of capital goods –

and examined their association with aggregate private investment. His estimates indicate, unsurprisingly, that uncertainty has an adverse direct impact on investment. This finding is particularly robust in the case of real exchange rate volatility, which invariably has a strongly negative effect on investment.

In 1997 the World Bank used a sample of 39 countries and found that those with low levels of corruption and high predictability of payments and outcomes achieved a ratio of gross investment to GDP of 28.5 per cent. Countries with high levels of corruption and low predictability of payments and outcomes achieved a ratio of only 12.3 per cent.[6]

But why should corruption affect investment decisions in this way? In fact the problem is much like the problem of 'information asymmetries' frequently cited by economists as leading to so-called market failure. Certain types of corruption lead to significant uncertainty as to whether the other side of a contract will be delivered or whether rights to accumulated capital and property will be secure. For example, if a small firm contracts with a large firm and delivers the agreed goods, but the large firm never pays for the goods and then bribes a corrupt judge to find in favour of it when payment is disputed, all business contracts in that environment become shrouded in uncertainty. Even apparently justly acquired property and capital might be reassigned to a different owner as a result of corrupt juridical processes. In such circumstances certain types of economic exchange can, in the extreme, dry up altogether. Long-term contracts are replaced by deals that are immediately settled for cash. Capital markets can cease to function and individuals can find that they have no security

---

6   *World Development Report 1997*, ch. 6, pp. 103–4.

against which to borrow money to start a business. Thus beneficial forms of exchange and contract never take place because of the uncertainty connected with them.

Society's morality and ethics decline

The three branches of government have defined roles. The legislature makes laws, the executive implements them and the judiciary enforces them. The fourth estate – the media – has a vital role in monitoring and reporting on the three branches of government, highlighting wrongdoing through investigative reporting.

Let us consider the four estates in turn and how they react to corruption. I have argued at the outset that corruption is infectious and contagious, so that when one sector becomes corrupt it affects the others. Society is weakened at its roots and the democratic process may be unable to cleanse corruption from society.

In terms of initiating corruption, the legislative branch is likely to be the most influential. Presidents and prime ministers have enormous powers of patronage, much of it overt and therefore uncorrupt, but some of it is covert too. They can appoint and sack ministers; some can appoint and sack senior functionaries and judges; all can make or break the careers of aspiring politicians.

If the legislative branch is corrupt, functionaries see what is occurring and realise that they can act similarly. Thus the executive branch becomes infected. The role of the judiciary then becomes pivotal. In the USA members of the Supreme Court are nominated by the president of the day but, once appointed by Congress, they have permanent tenure. This recognises the need for the judiciary to act as an essential constraint on the legislature and the executive.

The judiciary should be fully independent of the other two branches of government, but even in Western democracies including the UK and the USA politicians have some say in the appointment of judges. In the more corrupt developing countries, presidents openly remove judges who cause them trouble. This occurs, though less openly, in France and Italy. The magistrates and judges investigating the corruption scandals in the 1990s found huge opposing pressure from those in power, and ultimately some of the most tenacious and successful were forced to give up because of either exhaustion or harassment. As noted earlier, similar accounts are given by whistle-blowers in the European Commission.

The contagious nature of corruption enables it to cross readily from the legislature to the executive. If a minister, as part of the executive, decides that a contract shall be awarded to a particular firm that has paid a bribe, the functionaries will see clearly what is happening. If they are brave and if the service has a strong tradition of independence and integrity, it is possible that they may hold out against the minister, but only if they see this as a case in which their resistance will be supported at the highest level. When corruption has become the norm, there is no point in resisting. The minister may simply give an order or sack disobedient functionaries, or he may pass on to them some part of the bribe to gain their compliance.

Further down the hierarchy, when politicians and civil servants are corrupt, the police, customs officers and tax collectors follow suit. They may be badly paid and so feel that taking bribes is a perk of the job that is necessary for them to feed themselves and their families. There is a Russian saying: 'He who does not steal from the state is stealing from his family'. Note that stealing is not corruption under my definition, but the two are closely aligned in corrupt countries.

The role of the press and other media then becomes the primary or sole bastion against corruption, but only if the press itself is honest, independent and financially secure. Because of their power, the media are always at risk in corrupt countries. Even in uncorrupt countries ministers and politicians develop close relations with the media, feeding favoured journalists with stories, a practice taken to a high art by the current British Labour government.[7] Moreover, ministries have large advertising budgets.

In corrupt and despotic regimes such as those in Russia and Zimbabwe, journalists are intimidated and newspapers can be closed down by the government overnight. For example, in August, 2004 *Chechenskoye Obschestvo* (Chechen Society) was forced to close by the interior ministry office.[8] In February 2005 Jan Raath, one of the few remaining independent journalists in Harare, felt compelled to flee the country after escalating intimidation from the police. A tip-off from his lawyer warned him that his arrest was imminent.[9]

As Peters (2003) wrote, 'A difficult relationship between journalism and political power is a hallmark of democratic society.' Conversely, a cosy or docile relationship between the two is a recipe for the abuse of power in various ways, of which corruption may be one. The importance of independent journalism together with freedom of information cannot be overstated. When the media are no longer independent and free the public has no way

---

7   See Bower (2004), *passim.*
8   International Helsinki Federation for Human Rights, www.ihf-hr.org/welcome. php.
9   *The Times*, 19 February 2005, p. 7.

of knowing whether there is corruption at a high level. When they encounter corruption at a low level it is too late, because corruption percolates downwards through society. When corruption has reached the lower strata democracy itself is fatally flawed.

An example serves to show how corruption can all too readily become accepted by society once it has entered the system. A Ugandan schoolteacher of my acquaintance was spending a year taking a training course in the UK. I asked him whether he would have a job to go back to in Uganda. He explained that he was still being paid his full teacher's salary and would return to the same school when he had completed the course. The head teacher was fully aware that he was in the UK. His explanation was candid. To get a job in a state school he had had to bribe those making the appointment. This, he said, is standard practice. The bribe-takers keep bribes from those who do not get the job as well as from the successful applicant, so the cost to unsuccessful applicants is high. Having got the job, my friend had to keep it. He did not mention whether he had to bribe his head teacher for the latter's complicity in the matter. He spoke of corruption in Uganda without rancour and simply as part of the system. In the CPI 2004 Uganda ranks 102 out of 146.

Indeed, this example leads to another point. Those who are honest and uncorrupt have two options in such a system. They can partake in corruption to the extent necessary to carry on with the tasks of everyday life, or they can choose not to participate at all in the system. The former course of action leads to otherwise honest individuals themselves becoming part of the corrupt system. The latter course of action leads the uncorrupt person to suffer greatly, while leaving the economic system wholly in the hands of the corrupt. It is no wonder that corruption is contagious.

The corruptive impact of EU enlargement

As seen in the CPI 2004, important differences are found between the levels of perceived corruption in different EU member states (see Table 10). Within EU-15 Finland is the least corrupt state with a score of 9.7 and Greece is the most corrupt with 4.3. The average, weighted by population, was 7.36.

In 2004 EU-15 became EU-25. As the accession states have more corruption, other things being equal they increase the average level of corruption in EU-25. If we take the ten accession states and weight their CPI scores by population, their average is 4.37 compared with EU-15, whose average is 7.36. This means that the accession states increase the overall incidence of corruption in EU-25 and the new combined index number becomes 7.03. This is equivalent to an increase of 4.4 per cent in the average level of perceived corruption in the new EU-25.

More alarming is the prospect that four candidate states, two of them with large populations (Turkey, 70.7 million, and Romania, 22.3 million), may be permitted to join the EU. At present the average CPI score of those four states weighted by population is 3.22. If they were all to join the EU, other things being equal the EU's overall corruption score will fall to 6.28. This means that they will increase corruption in EU-29 by a further 10.2 per cent.

We do not know what happens when a relatively corrupt group of nations merges with another less corrupt group. Does the new corrupt group increase corruption in the formerly less corrupt group? Does the less corrupt group cleanse the more corrupt group? Or does corruption in the newly enlarged group converge at the average level of corruption weighted by population?

Table 10 **Impact of EU enlargement on the overall level of perceived corruption, 2005**

	CPI 2004	Pop. million	% of pop.	CPI weighted by population		
				EU-15	EU-25	EU-29
Austria	8.4	8.1	2.1	0.18	0.16	0.13
Belgium	7.5	10.4	2.7	0.20	0.18	0.15
Denmark	9.5	5.4	1.4	0.13	0.12	0.10
Finland	9.7	5.2	1.4	0.13	0.12	0.09
France	7.1	61.5	16.1	1.14	1.02	0.82
Germany	8.2	82.5	21.5	1.77	1.57	1.26
Greece	4.3	11.0	2.9	0.12	0.11	0.09
Ireland	7.5	4.0	1.0	0.08	0.07	0.06
Italy	4.8	57.3	15.0	0.72	0.64	0.51
Luxembourg	8.4	0.5	0.1	0.01	0.01	0.01
Netherlands	8.7	16.2	4.2	0.37	0.33	0.26
Portugal	6.3	10.4	2.7	0.17	0.15	0.12
Spain	7.1	41.6	10.8	0.77	0.69	0.55
Sweden	9.2	8.9	2.3	0.21	0.19	0.15
UK	8.6	60.3	15.7	1.35	1.21	0.97
EU-15		**383.3**	**100.0**	**7.36**	**6.56**	**5.27**
Accession states						
Cyprus	5.4	0.8	1.7	0.09	0.01	0.01
Czech Republic	4.2	10.2	22.0	0.92	0.10	0.08
Estonia	6.0	1.4	2.9	0.18	0.02	0.02
Hungary	4.8	10.1	21.8	1.05	0.11	0.09
Latvia	4.6	2.3	5.0	0.23	0.03	0.02
Lithuania	4.6	3.5	7.5	0.34	0.04	0.03
Malta	6.8	0.4	0.9	0.06	0.01	0.01
Poland	3.5	10.4	22.4	0.78	0.08	0.07
Slovakia	4.0	5.4	11.6	0.46	0.05	0.04
Slovenia	6.0	2.0	4.3	0.26	0.03	0.02
Accession states		46.5	100.0	4.37	0.47	0.38
EU-25					**7.03**	
Candidate states						
Bulgaria	4.1	8.0	7.6	0.31		0.06
Croatia	3.5	4.5	4.2	0.15		0.03
Romania	2.9	22.3	21.1	0.61		0.12
Turkey	3.2	70.7	67.1	2.15		0.42
Candidate states		105.4	100.0	3.22		0.63
EU-29						**6.28**

Summary	CPI	Index
EU-15, 2004	7.36	100.0
EU-25, 2004	7.03	95.6
EU-29, 2007?	6.28	85.4

* Weighted by population
Table: Ian Senior

It is worth noting that the EU structures of governance allow corruption from one source to infect it easily. There are commissioners from the more corrupt new members and, in the future, from candidate states, who have complete executive responsibility for whole areas of policy throughout the EU, only partially restrained by the democratic accountability of the European Parliament. This itself is a weak body with a record for exploiting bountiful tax-free perquisites.

It is also certain that if corruption continues in the European Commission itself, the prospect of reducing corruption in the member states has little hope of success. In particular, the growing corruption in Germany coupled with historically endemic corruption in France, Italy and Spain gives cause for concern and suggests that closer political ties within the EU under a new constitution may enhance corruption in the UK. In particular, it seems wrong to hand further power to a European Commission whose accounts for a decade have been qualified by its auditors, whose MEPs openly claim artificially inflated expenses and whose whistle-blowers get hounded out of their jobs. The UK should reject any new EU constitution that strengthens the powers of the European Commission, its elected members and its functionaries until the entire project has been cleansed of the corruption that currently prevails.

6 CURES FOR CORRUPTION

General

Attitudes towards anti-social behaviour develop during child-hood. They begin with parenting and continue with experience at school. The concept of corruption as a crime, however, is for adults — nobody will have been told this by their parents or teachers — but it seems plausible that young people who have learned that stealing is wrong will later accept that corruption is wrong too. The difficulty arises when complete societies have come to consider stealing from the state, if not from each other, to be normal and acceptable.

From the earlier chapters we have seen that corruption has become ingrained in some societies, whether it is for gaining entry to a state university in Russia or paying a policeman to avoid a faked traffic offence in Kenya. When corruption is endemic the starting point becomes: 'If I don't offer a bribe when everyone else is doing so, I won't obtain the licence/contract/university place.' Therefore the bribe becomes a form of taxation that must be paid, and the concept of corruption as a crime has been lost.

The principal people who can change a culture of corruption if they wish to do so are politicians. This is because they make the laws and allocate the funds that enable laws to be enforced. If, however, politicians at the top of the hierarchy have routinely worked their way up by accepting bribes to fund their parties and themselves, there is little prospect that they will wish to cleanse their colleagues or their nation of corruption. Those who have paid and received bribes know of too much dirty linen. If their party depends on corrupt donations, their aim is to garner donations as much as they wish to garner votes.

A fully functional democracy is the most effective way of enabling voters to get rid of corrupt politicians. John Major's Conservative government was tainted with 'sleaze', part of which related to corruption as I have defined it, and sleaze was a significant campaign issue for New Labour in 1997. In the almost bloodless revolutions that have taken place in Azerbaijan, Belarus, Georgia, Ukraine and Uzbekistan the corruption of incumbent administrations has always been a significant issue. As noted earlier, in Canada in 2006 the ousting of the Liberals from government was strongly influenced by allegations of sleaze that were levelled at the former prime minister and those close to him. Only when politicians recognise that to be *uncorrupt* is a vote-winner will they wake up as a group. If individual politicians lose office or go to jail for corruption, 'uncorruption' will be seen as a political benefit that outweighs the short-term attraction of bulging brown-paper envelopes.

When politicians promise to rid the state of corruption, those who are compelled to pay bribes, as in Kenya and Uganda, instanced above, are being offered a significant cut in 'taxes', which is always a vote-winner.

It is unfortunate that electoral systems in corrupt states such as Zimbabwe are so easy to manipulate. Even if the electorate votes for candidates who will free them from the scourge of corruption, the same candidates may be artificially debarred from power by the despot of the day. When, as in Kenya, a new administration is elected on the promise to rid the country of corruption, and then within months becomes provenly corrupt, the electorate has been thwarted yet again.

In wholly corrupt countries there is little scope for individuals to fight corruption. By contrast there is considerable scope for international agencies to do so. Where developing countries are dependent on foreign aid the international agencies or foreign countries can require corrupt states to cleanse their systems before aid is given. Particularly in the case of international agencies, however, this in turn requires that the agencies themselves be uncorrupt.

The oil-for-food corruption scandal at the United Nations' headquarters is of high concern. Following the Volcker inquiry we must hope that there were only a few rotten apples in the barrel rather than something more widespread.

Corruption in the European Commission, an institution that grants massive funds to Third World nations as well as to member states, must be a matter of concern to those who wish to rid the world of corruption. It is noticeable that the EC's internal corruption is habitually ignored or glossed over by those politicians who advocate a new constitution leading to the United States of Europe with increased powers for the Commission as an institution and for the commissioners over whom the weak, elected European Parliament has little control.

It is also worth mentioning that government-to-government aid to a corrupt country can support the institutions that harbour corruption. It can also lead to greater potential for government preferment by increasing the economic resources that are directly controlled by a government, thus making a potential corruptor's actions worthwhile.

The recipe for cleansing a state begins thus: 'First find a completely uncorrupt politician and make him president or prime minister, whichever is the position of executive authority. Then let him appoint a cabinet of other ministers who also are untainted by corruption. Next pass laws that give freedom to the press, provide heavy penalties for proven corruption, give protection to whistle-blowers, and dismiss on the spot any minister, law-maker or functionary found to be corrupt'. It is as simple at that … in theory!

In practice, it is otherwise. The very people who are the greatest beneficiaries of corruption have the greatest power and use the corrupt nature of government to maintain that power.

To find an entirely uncorrupt prime minister, even in western Europe, is hard. John Major in the UK may have been one such. He had a tiny majority during his years in office, however, and was unable to apply swift and decisive retribution when needed. Further, his 'back to basics' campaign backfired because of its failure to distinguish between ministers having mistresses and ministers who had accepted covert money in their roles as politicians.

Tony Blair's 1997 election campaign benefited enormously from the optimism that his would truly be an uncorrupt regime. For this reason, the scandal of Bernie Ecclestone's payment to the Labour Party in return, seemingly, for favourable treatment of Formula One's receipt of tobacco advertising was jarring. Similarly, the 'loans-for-peerages' row, which is unresolved at the time of going to press and in which Tony Blair has been involved for the Labour Party, may prove a factor as far ahead as the next general election.

To find an uncorrupt prime minister and ministers from a fully corrupted political system may be an impossible requirement. In sub-Saharan Africa and many other parts of the world, including France, the established tradition is that politicians expect enrichment from office. They enter politics with this in mind and, having attained office, they expect not just to enrich themselves but to pay back their supporters as well, particularly in the tribal context of Africa. President Mugabe gave the white farms he had seized to his family, cronies and members of his political party. These spoils of power exemplify what happens in corrupt states where property rights are overruled by dictatorship.

When occasionally an African opposition party comes to power with a commitment to fight corruption, the most uncorrupt Western democracies, notably those in Scandinavia, should be employed to train investigators and accountants to help them root out corruption. In this context France, Germany, Italy and Spain could finance the Scandinavian projects, but their expertise, if any, in dealing with corruption should be declined. Zimbabwe will be a case in point when President Mugabe is finally ousted. African leaders must, however, genuinely commit to uncorruption. To politicians in opposition words come easy.

The experience of Kenya is particularly discouraging. The government of Daniel Arap Moi was so corrupt and oppressive that from time to time the World Bank cut off funding for aid projects. This produced short-term changes but stopped far short of eradicating corruption. When the government of President Mwai Kibaki came to power in 2002 it did so principally on the promise to get rid of corruption, but corruption continued. The British high commissioner to Kenya, Edward Clay, has publicly said that Kibaki has failed to prevent 'massive looting' of public funds.

In February 2005 two officials who had been given the specific task of cleansing Kenya of corruption resigned within a short time of each other, saying that they did not have the means to do the work. One of them, John Githongo, left his pivotal position of Permanent Secretary for Governance and Ethics under the Office of the President when he found that his inquiries were leading him to such high places that his life was in danger. He fled to the UK.

Transparency

The most effective way of putting international pressure on corrupt, pauper nations is for aid to be available only to those that are demonstrably rooting out corruption. Countries with corrupt governments should be excluded from all aid programmes and soft loans. Their international debts should not be cancelled.

Codes must be adopted to make the revenues of politicians and senior functionaries everywhere fully transparent. All monetary gifts and the value of favours in kind above a certain level must be itemised for public scrutiny. A failure to make a correct return would mean disbarment from public office. In properly working democracies with a free press all concerned have an incentive to scrutinise their opponents' financial declarations and to look for commissions and omissions.

The reporting threshold of values for gifts and favours received by politicians should be set low. In industrialised countries the threshold for declarable gifts and favours to individual politicians should be set at £1,000 per annum from each source. In developing countries the figure would be reduced in accordance with purchasing power or levels of income per head. Gifts between office holders in their official capacity, for example between heads of state, should be handed over to museums or auctioned, with the proceeds going to the Revenue. Gifts to functionaries should be banned completely.

Political parties at local and national level must be required to publish full lists of donations received from companies and individuals, all by name. Anonymous donations above £1,000 should be illegal. Electoral commissions such as that of the UK would have the obligation to conduct snap audits on political parties nationally and locally.

The UK has made progress in this direction. The gifts of millions of pounds that the Conservative and Labour parties solicit and receive now have to be declared. Even the Liberal Democrats have recently been tarnished by taking a gift of over £2 million from a donor who does not reside in the UK, does not pay taxes here and cannot vote. These gifts are not corrupt because they have to be declared to the Electoral Commission and thus are overt. Even so, they raise the question of whether and how donors influence the parties that receive their largesse. As noted earlier, the loophole of providing loans, even if on supposedly commercial terms, must be closed by making the loans and their terms fully transparent.

Cutting the supply of bribes at source

Transparency International's annual reports provide details of corruption around the world and the actions that some governments are taking to combat it. We must hope that the governments of corrupt countries, having been named, feel shamed into action. But shaming is not enough. It must be accompanied by the immediate cutting off of international aid, including soft loans, to those countries in which corruption is prevalent. Any country that scores 3 or less in the CPI 2004 and subsequent editions should have its international aid cut off until it can show that it is taking effective measures to root out corruption and, crucially, has a free press.

Further, international funds must be channelled only through international and local agencies that themselves are transparently free from corruption. Any agency in which corruption arises, starting with the UN secretariat and the European Commission, should see its head functionary removed automatically from his or her post.

New sanctions must be imposed on firms that use bribes to win contracts, whether at home or abroad. For many years Western firms bidding for civil engineering, construction, defence or equipment projects in Third World countries have judged that if other bidders were offering bribes they would have to do so too. In some countries the cost of bribes in export contracts may still be allowed by the tax authorities as a legitimate expense. This must end.

Governments should use a powerful tool at their disposal. The companies that are found to have used bribes to gain export contracts, both at home and abroad, should be excluded from national government contracts for five years and additionally from any government-backed export credit guarantee schemes. The countries receiving the bribe should have bilateral aid programmes suspended until action against the corrupting firm or individual has been taken.

This powerful sanction should be adopted specifically by the 21 big exporting countries listed in TI's Bribe Payers' Index 2002

Table 11 **Bribe Payers' Index, 2002,* compared with the Corruption Perceptions Index, 2004**

Ranked by BPI	Country	Score	
		BPI	CPI
1	Australia	8.5	8.8
2	Sweden	8.4	9.2
	Switzerland	8.4	9.1
4	Austria	8.2	8.4
5	Canada	8.1	8.5
6	Netherlands	7.8	8.7
	Belgium	7.8	7.5
8	United Kingdom	6.9	8.6
9	Singapore	6.3	9.3
	Germany	6.3	8.2
11	Spain	5.8	7.1
12	France	5.5	7.1
13	USA	5.3	7.5
	Japan	5.3	6.9
15	Malaysia	4.3	5.0
	Hong Kong	4.3	8.0
17	Italy	4.1	4.8
18	South Korea	3.9	4.5
19	Taiwan	3.8	5.6
20	People's Republic of China	3.5	3.4
21	Russia	3.2	2.8

*This is the most recent edition.
Note: 10.0 = lowest propensity to bribe, 0 = highest propensity to bribe
Table: Ian Senior, from Transparency International data

(Galtung, 2003).[1] The index was based on surveys conducted by Gallup International Association in fifteen emerging market economies. Its aim was to establish which exporting countries and which industries were most likely to offer bribes. The results are shown in Table 11. I have added the CPI score for each country

---

1   www.transparency.org/pressreleases_archive/2002/2002.05.14.bpi.en.html.

in 2004. The correlation between the CPI and the Bribe Payers' Index (the R^2) is 0.72, and the t-statistic of significance is high at 7.06. This suggests that there is a significant relationship between countries' levels of internal corruption generally and their propensity to offer bribes in international trade.

Encouraging whistle-blowing

It is hard to imagine that anyone enjoys whistle-blowing. It may lead to the loss of promotion prospects, the loss of a job or ostracism within the workplace. Organisations may turn savagely against the whistle-blower. The case of Dr David Kelly will be remembered. He believed that the British government's case for going to war with Iraq had overstated the threat of weapons of mass destruction and he leaked his opinion to Andrew Gilligan, a BBC reporter. Both were hounded by the government. No weapons of mass destruction were found so they were both vindicated. By then Dr Kelly had committed suicide and Andrew Gilligan had left the BBC, though he may not have been formally sacked.

For any whistle-blower it is essential to name names and to have hard evidence to support claims. This entails, in effect, spying on colleagues. Further, the whistle-blower must expect that those whom he accuses of corruption will not only deny it but will produce counter-charges against him. He runs a double risk: failing to prove his case and ruining his career.

Governments that sincerely wish to clamp down on corruption and indeed on other forms of crime need to protect and encourage whistle-blowers. For many years the USA has had whistle-blower legislation in the form of the False Claims Act. This was designed to cut out false claims by contractors to the federal and state governments. In 1986 Congress added anti-retaliation protection for whistle-blowers, as well as granting them a percentage of the money saved or retrieved by the state as a result of their information.

In the UK the Labour government has run campaigns encouraging people to ring a confidential telephone number and inform on others whom they believe to be falsely claiming social security benefits. It is uncertain what results these campaigns have had.

Whistle-blowing and informing are contentious. There are awkward parallels with Nazi Germany, in which citizens were encouraged to inform the Gestapo where Jews were hiding; with Ceausescu's Romania, in which 15 per cent of the population were on the payroll as informants of the Securitate, the secret police; and with North Korea today, where nobody dares speak ill anywhere of the Dear Leader, Kim Il Jung.

In Japan there is a deeply entrenched ethos of loyalty to the company, which historically provides security and a job for life. Whistle-blowing is particularly reviled. A recent court case awarded the employee of a large haulage company, Hiroaki Kushioka, £70,000 in damages. In 1974 he went public about his company's involvement in illegal cartels. He was immediately moved to a hut with a small desk and nothing on it. Since then, for 30 years he has had nothing to do except occasional menial tasks such as weeding the car park. Every day his superior harangues him, telling him to resign. He refuses, believing that as a whistle-blower he is now unemployable elsewhere.[2] By British standards Kushioka's award is a pittance for the mental anguish and loss of earnings he has experienced. It may have a wider significance,

2   *The Times*, 26 February 2005.

however, if it serves as a legal precedent for other 'disgraced' employees who, in Japanese terminology, have been condemned to 'watch the window' for whistle-blowing.

Somewhere a balance must be struck between Ceausescu's ubiquitous network of informants and the Japanese view that whistle-blowing is the ultimate betrayal of corporate loyalty. The best way to look at whistle-blowing is as just one tool, and preferably a diminishing one, in a government's set of instruments to combat and eliminate corruption.

Corporate culture can and must be changed in all sectors, both public and private. Women in the workplace have for generations suffered sexist harassment, glass ceilings and lower pay than male colleagues. Courts are now awarding damages in cases of sexual discrimination which would make Mr Kushioka's £70,000 for 30 years of harassment seem paltry. Senior managers and public figures such as Ruud Lubbers, formerly UN High Commissioner for Refugees, have been forced to resign for sexist actions. If corporate culture can change in this area, it can change with regard to attitudes to corruption too.

In the UK investigative reporting is a strongly established and respected activity. By far and away the most courageous and diligent title is *Private Eye*, which for 40 years has been a conduit for well-informed stories about corruption at national and local level. These stories are copiously detailed, and it is now seldom that those named sue for libel. The magazine's circulation is 200,000 and it has far outstripped other papers in exposing political dishonesty and corruption. *Private Eye* and France's *Le Canard Enchaîné* play a vital part in providing a conduit for well-informed accounts of corruption in both the public and private sectors.

Zero tolerance of corruption, particularly political corruption

Uncorruption must start at the highest political level with no exemptions and zero tolerance. In France the president is immune from prosecution for any criminal acts, including corruption during his tenure of office. This immunity should be removed. It is particularly important that presidents, prime ministers and politicians at all levels should be transparently uncorrupt.

Well-documented cases of corruption at a high political level make citizens cynical and breed the feeling that if the politicians can do it, why shouldn't we? And, as mentioned above, corruption is much harder to root out at lower levels once it infects higher levels. Zero tolerance should be a reality, not just a sound bite.

Corruption and free markets

It has already been noted in Chapter 4 that there was no positive statistical relationship between most measures of government intervention and corruption. Some measures of government intervention simply did not produce a significant relationship at all (for example, variables relating to government involvement in trade and inward investment). Counter-intuitively, one measure of government intervention gave rise to a significant negative relationship with corruption. More intuitively, the amount of regulation and corruption were positively related. I have already commented on the limitations of the statistical aspects of this analysis.

At an intuitive level it would seem difficult to argue that removing government involvement altogether from sectors of the economy such as trade and inward and outward investment could do anything but reduce opportunities for corruption. Certainly, foreign trade transactions are a major source of corrupt activity in countries where such transactions are regulated. Other forms of government intervention (high taxes, rigid employment regulations and so on) may also lead to corruption unless the basic structures of government are very sound with an independent judiciary, free press and a high degree of honesty in society. Thus the reduction of regulation, particularly the sort of burdensome regulation that appears to have no purpose and which individuals feel no guilt about avoiding by paying bribes, would seem to be a measure that should help reduce corruption as well as helping the economy in other ways.

7   CONCLUSION

Summary of the argument

I began by exploring definitions of corruption. My definition of corruption is new and does not derive from those that have gone before. It is independent of time, place, legislation and moral codes. It also defines a given act as corrupt regardless of whether a government official or the public sector is involved in some way. This is important because the government sector is itself sometimes difficult to define. Economists and sociologists who write papers about corruption but who do not define the word should have their papers rejected.

I have shown that corruption is widespread in western Europe, as well as in the developing world. It is not confined to the governments of specific countries – there are significant examples of corruption in the EC and the UN. The vast majority of identified corruption does, though, involve government.

It is clear from the analysis of data that corruption and dishonesty go hand in hand. Some other statistical relationships between corruption and economic variables were, however, counter-intuitive. For example, corruption seems to increase as government intervention decreases. Possible reasons for this have been discussed in the relevant chapters.

It is clear that corruption goes hand in hand with low

economic growth and I have identified reasons why corruption can undermine the market economy. Corruption can also subvert the honesty and integrity of society more generally. Curing corruption is difficult. In a corrupt society, the very people who are in a position to cure society of corruption benefit most from it. Even the democratic process has mixed success in developing uncorrupt governments out of corrupt governments. A corrupt government can, of course, corrupt the democratic process itself; a newly elected uncorrupt government can quickly find itself out of its depth in fighting corruption. Perhaps the best hope of defeating corruption is pressure from other governments, particularly where those other governments are providing a corrupt government with economic aid.

Zero tolerance of corruption

Economists need to press the case that I and others have made that corruption is *inefficient*. The prices paid in a society in which corruption is endemic do not allocate resources efficiently. If bidders for government or private contracts pay more than necessary because of bribes, the state or other purchaser gets less value than in an uncorrupt society. The corruptee in turn is likely to bank his bribes in Switzerland against a rainy day. Ultimately corruption can undermine a market economy at its foundations if security of contract and property is undermined by a corrupt judiciary. Once the miasma of corruption has descended over a country the cost of capital increases and the willingness of investors to invest falls. In the extreme, economic life, apart from basic transactions in the cash economy, can grind to a halt. In time people at all levels learn to live with corruption and merely shrug their shoulders when a president is ousted in a coup and flees to a safe haven with a luxury villa paid for from his Swiss bank account.

Corruption distorts the allocation of wealth within society. It channels bribes upwards to the wealthy, into government structures and then out to individuals working within those structures. It becomes a tax on the lowest layers of society, who have no way of receiving bribes to compensate for those they have paid. This is particularly obnoxious in developing countries with poor health, poor education, short life expectancy and substantial malnourishment. For years the UN and aid agencies have wrung their hands over endemic corruption in recipient states but have done little about it. The new policy should be one of zero tolerance. Aid should be given only to countries that independent audits show to be uncorrupt. Lofty words about helping poverty in Africa and elsewhere should be replaced by hard actions that require externally monitored fair elections, the externally audited use of aid funds and a completely free press.

Markets working with undistorted price signals enable individuals to choose the products and services that best satisfy their needs. This is the working of Adam Smith's 'invisible hand'. Corruption is a disease that cripples the hand. Those who believe that corruption is to be accepted in developing countries if it oils an otherwise creaking system need to think again.

In the UK we have led the world in liberalising markets. Our record on dealing with corruption is better than many, and our ranking in the Corruption Perceptions Index has been consistently high. Nevertheless, we must improve internally so that we can demonstrate to corrupt countries by example that *uncorruption* pays.

REFERENCES

Alam, M. S. (1989), 'Anatomy of corruption: an approach to the political economy of underdevelopment', *American Journal of Economics and Sociology*, 48(4): 441–56.

Beach, W. W. and M. A. Miles (2005), 'Explaining the factors of *The Index of Economic Freedom*'.

Bower, T. (2004), *Gordon Brown*, London: HarperCollins.

Felten, E. (2001), 'Finders keepers', *Reader's Digest*, April.

Frei, M. (2005), *Getting the Boot. Italy's Unfinished Revolution*, London: Times Books.

Galtung, F. (2003), 'Bribe payers' index', in Transparency International, *Global Corruption Report*, London: Profile Books, pp. 266–8.

Heidenheimer, A. J. (1989), 'Perspectives on the perception of corruption', in A. J. Heidenheimer, M. Johnston and V. Le Vine (eds), *Political Corruption: A Handbook*, New Brunswick, NJ, p. 161.

Hutchcroft, P. D. (1997), 'The politics of privilege: assessing the impact of rents, corruption, and clientelism on Third World development', *Political Studies*, XLV: 639–58.

Ignatius, D. (2002), 'True crime: the scent of French scandal', www.legalaffairs.org/issues/May-June-2002/story_ignatius_mayjun2002.htm.

Johnson, R. A. (2004), 'The United States', in R. A. Johnson (ed.), *The Struggle against Corruption: A Comparative Study*, New York: Palgrave Macmillan.

Johnson, R. A. and S. Sharma (2004), 'About corruption', in R. A. Johnson (ed.), *The Struggle against Corruption: A Comparative Study*, New York: Palgrave Macmillan.

Jones, T. (2003), *The Dark Heart of Italy*, New York: North Point Press.

Kalchheim, C. (2004), 'White corruption in Israel', in R. A. Johnson (ed.), *The Struggle against Corruption: A Comparative Study*, New York: Palgrave Macmillan, p. 70.

Kaufmann, D. and S.-J. Wei (1999), 'Does "grease money" speed up the wheels of commerce?',World Bank Country Economics Department, December, http://netec.mcc.ac.uk/BibEc/data/Papers/fthwobaco2254.html.

King, T. (2004), 'French favours'. *Prospect*, January, pp. 24–31.

Martirossian, J. (2004), 'Russia and her ghosts of the past', in R. A. Johnson (ed.), *The Struggle against Corruption: A Comparative Study*, New York: Palgrave Macmillan, pp. 81–108.

Mati, M. and W. Mwangi (2003), in Transparency International, *Global Corruption Report*, London: Profile Books, p. 242.

Meadowcroft, J. and J. Blundell (2004), 'The Morecambe Bay cockle pickers: market failure or government disaster?', *Economic Affairs*, 24(3): 69–71.

Miles, M. A., E. J. Feulner, M. A. O'Grady et al. (2005), *The Index of Economic Freedom: The link between economic opportunity and prosperity*, Washington, DC/New York: Heritage Foundation/Wall Street Journal.

Mitchell, R. H. (1996), *Political Bribery in Japan*, University of Hawaii Press.

Neild, R. (2002), *Public Corruption: The Dark Side of the Social Revolution*, London: Anthem Press.

Nye, J. S. (1967), 'Corruption and political development: a cost–benefit analysis', *American Political Science Review*, LXI(2): 417–27.

OLAF (2003/04), Annual report.

Open Society Institute (2002), *Monitoring the EU Accession Process: Corruption and Anti-corruption Policy*.

Peters, B. (2003), 'The media's role: covering or covering up corruption', in Transparency International, *Global Corruption Report*, London: Profile Books, p. 44.

Senior, I. (1998), 'An economic view of corruption', *Journal of Interdisciplinary Economics*, 9: 145–61.

Senior, I. (2004), 'Corruption, the government and the private sector: why it matters and what can be done', *Economic Affairs*, 24(2): 22–9.

Serven, L. (1998), 'Macroeconomic uncertainty and private investment in developing countries: an empirical investigation', Policy Research Working Paper Series no. 2035, World Bank.

Shelley, L. I. (1997), 'Post-Soviet organised crime: a new form of authoritarianism', in P. Williams (ed.), *Russian Organised Crime: The New Threat?*, Portland, OR: Frank Cass.

Sterling, C. (1994), *Crime without Frontiers*, London: Little, Brown.

Sussman, L. R., K. Guida et al. (2003), *How Free? The Web & the Press: The Annual Survey of Press Freedom*, Freedom House.

Theobald, R. (1999), 'So what really is the problem about corruption?', *Third World Quarterly*, 20(3): 491–502.

Tzilivakis, K. (2003), *Athens News*, 10 January.

UNDP PARAGON Generic Training Module on Public Service Ethics and Accountability. Italy: G 05B, http://unpan1.un.org/intradoc/groups/public/documents/eropa/unpan002688.pdf.

Van Hove, L. (1997), Doctoral thesis, Vrije Universiteit, Brussels, reported on www.expatica.com, 4 March.

Waterbury, J. (1973), 'Endemic and planned corruption in a monarchical regime', *World Politics*, XXV(4): 533–5.

Williams, R. J. (1976), 'The problem of corruption: a conceptual and comparative analysis', *PAC Bulletin*, 22: 41–53.

Williams, R. J. (1999), 'New concepts for old?', *Third World Quarterly*, 20(3): 503–13.

Williams, R. J. (ed.) (2000), *Explaining Corruption*, vol. 1, Cheltenham: Edward Elgar.

Williams, R., R. Theobald, J. Moran, R. Flanary and A. Doig (eds) (2000), *The Politics of Corruption*, 4 vols, Cheltenham/Northampton, MA: Edward Elgar.

World Development Report (1997).

ABOUT THE IEA

The Institute is a research and educational charity (No. CC 235 351), limited by guarantee. Its mission is to improve understanding of the fundamental institutions of a free society with particular reference to the role of markets in solving economic and social problems.

The IEA achieves its mission by:

- a high-quality publishing programme
- conferences, seminars, lectures and other events
- outreach to school and college students
- brokering media introductions and appearances

The IEA, which was established in 1955 by the late Sir Antony Fisher, is an educational charity, not a political organisation. It is independent of any political party or group and does not carry on activities intended to affect support for any political party or candidate in any election or referendum, or at any other time. It is financed by sales of publications, conference fees and voluntary donations.

In addition to its main series of publications the IEA also publishes a quarterly journal, *Economic Affairs*.

The IEA is aided in its work by a distinguished international Academic Advisory Council and an eminent panel of Honorary Fellows. Together with other academics, they review prospective IEA publications, their comments being passed on anonymously to authors. All IEA papers are therefore subject to the same rigorous independent refereeing process as used by leading academic journals.

IEA publications enjoy widespread classroom use and course adoptions in schools and universities. They are also sold throughout the world and often translated/reprinted.

Since 1974 the IEA has helped to create a world-wide network of 100 similar institutions in over 70 countries. They are all independent but share the IEA's mission.

Views expressed in the IEA's publications are those of the authors, not those of the Institute (which has no corporate view), its Managing Trustees, Academic Advisory Council members or senior staff.

Members of the Institute's Academic Advisory Council, Honorary Fellows, Trustees and Staff are listed on the following page.

The Institute gratefully acknowledges financial support for its publications programme and other work from a generous benefaction by the late Alec and Beryl Warren.

Other papers recently published by the IEA include:

WHO, What and Why?

Transnational Government, Legitimacy and the World Health Organization
Roger Scruton
Occasional Paper 113; ISBN 0 255 36487 3
£8.00

The World Turned Rightside Up

A New Trading Agenda for the Age of Globalisation
John C. Hulsman
Occasional Paper 114; ISBN 0 255 36495 4
£8.00

The Representation of Business in English Literature

Introduced and edited by Arthur Pollard
Readings 53; ISBN 0 255 36491 1
£12.00

Anti-Liberalism 2000

The Rise of New Millennium Collectivism
David Henderson
Occasional Paper 115; ISBN 0 255 36497 0
£7.50

Capitalism, Morality and Markets

Brian Griffiths, Robert A. Sirico, Norman Barry & Frank Field
Readings 54; ISBN 0 255 36496 2
£7.50

A Conversation with Harris and Seldon

Ralph Harris & Arthur Seldon

Occasional Paper 116; ISBN 0 255 36498 9

£7.50

Malaria and the DDT Story

Richard Tren & Roger Bate

Occasional Paper 117; ISBN 0 255 36499 7

£10.00

A Plea to Economists Who Favour Liberty: Assist the Everyman

Daniel B. Klein

Occasional Paper 118; ISBN 0 255 36501 2

£10.00

The Changing Fortunes of Economic Liberalism

Yesterday, Today and Tomorrow

David Henderson

Occasional Paper 105 (new edition); ISBN 0 255 36520 9

£12.50

The Global Education Industry

Lessons from Private Education in Developing Countries

James Tooley

Hobart Paper 141 (new edition); ISBN 0 255 36503 9

£12.50

Saving Our Streams

The Role of the Anglers' Conservation Association in
Protecting English and Welsh Rivers
Roger Bate
Research Monograph 53; ISBN 0 255 36494 6
£10.00

Better Off Out?

The Benefits or Costs of EU Membership
Brian Hindley & Martin Howe
Occasional Paper 99 (new edition); ISBN 0 255 36502 0
£10.00

Buckingham at 25

Freeing the Universities from State Control
Edited by James Tooley
Readings 55; ISBN 0 255 36512 8
£15.00

Lectures on Regulatory and Competition Policy

Irwin M. Stelzer
Occasional Paper 120; ISBN 0 255 36511 X
,12.50

Misguided Virtue

False Notions of Corporate Social Responsibility
David Henderson
Hobart Paper 142; ISBN 0 255 36510 1
£12.50

HIV and Aids in Schools

The Political Economy of Pressure Groups and Miseducation
Barrie Craven, Pauline Dixon, Gordon Stewart & James Tooley
Occasional Paper 121; ISBN 0 255 36522 5
£10.00

The Road to Serfdom

The Reader's Digest *condensed version*
Friedrich A. Hayek
Occasional Paper 122; ISBN 0 255 36530 6
£7.50

Bastiat's *The Law*

Introduction by Norman Barry
Occasional Paper 123; ISBN 0 255 36509 8
£7.50

A Globalist Manifesto for Public Policy

Charles Calomiris
Occasional Paper 124; ISBN 0 255 36525 x
£7.50

Euthanasia for Death Duties

Putting Inheritance Tax Out of Its Misery
Barry Bracewell-Milnes
Research Monograph 54; ISBN 0 255 36513 6
£10.00

Liberating the Land
The Case for Private Land-use Planning
Mark Pennington
Hobart Paper 143; ISBN 0 255 36508 x
£10.00

IEA Yearbook of Government Performance 2002/2003
Edited by Peter Warburton
Yearbook 1; ISBN 0 255 36532 2
£15.00

Britain's Relative Economic Performance, 1870–1999
Nicholas Crafts
Research Monograph 55; ISBN 0 255 36524 1
£10.00

Should We Have Faith in Central Banks?
Otmar Issing
Occasional Paper 125; ISBN 0 255 36528 4
£7.50

The Dilemma of Democracy
Arthur Seldon
Hobart Paper 136 (reissue); ISBN 0 255 36536 5
£10.00

Capital Controls: a 'Cure' Worse Than the Problem?
Forrest Capie
Research Monograph 56; ISBN 0 255 36506 3
£10.00

The Poverty of 'Development Economics'
Deepak Lal
Hobart Paper 144 (reissue); ISBN 0 255 36519 5
£15.00

Should Britain Join the Euro?
The Chancellor's Five Tests Examined
Patrick Minford
Occasional Paper 126; ISBN 0 255 36527 6
£7.50

Post-Communist Transition: Some Lessons
Leszek Balcerowicz
Occasional Paper 127; ISBN 0 255 36533 0
£7.50

A Tribute to Peter Bauer
John Blundell et al.
Occasional Paper 128; ISBN 0 255 36531 4
£10.00

Employment Tribunals
Their Growth and the Case for Radical Reform
J. R. Shackleton
Hobart Paper 145; ISBN 0 255 36515 2
£10.00

Fifty Economic Fallacies Exposed
Geoffrey E. Wood
Occasional Paper 129; ISBN 0 255 36518 7
£12.50

A Market in Airport Slots
Keith Boyfield (editor), David Starkie, Tom Bass & Barry Humphreys
Readings 56; ISBN 0 255 36505 5
£10.00

Money, Inflation and the Constitutional Position of the Central Bank
Milton Friedman & Charles A. E. Goodhart
Readings 57; ISBN 0 255 36538 1
£10.00

railway.com
Parallels between the Early British Railways and the ICT Revolution
Robert C. B. Miller
Research Monograph 57; ISBN 0 255 36534 9
£12.50

The Regulation of Financial Markets
Edited by Philip Booth & David Currie
Readings 58; ISBN 0 255 36551 9
£12.50

Climate Alarmism Reconsidered
Robert L. Bradley Jr
Hobart Paper 146; ISBN 0 255 36541 1
£12.50

Government Failure: E. G. West on Education
Edited by James Tooley & James Stanfield
Occasional Paper 130; ISBN 0 255 36552 7
£12.50

Waging the War of Ideas
John Blundell
Second edition
Occasional Paper 131; ISBN 0 255 36547 0
£12.50

Corporate Governance: Accountability in the Marketplace
Elaine Sternberg
Second edition
Hobart Paper 147; ISBN 0 255 36542 x
£12.50

The Land Use Planning System
Evaluating Options for Reform
John Corkindale
Hobart Paper 148; ISBN 0 255 36550 0
£10.00

Economy and Virtue

Essays on the Theme of Markets and Morality
Edited by Dennis O'Keeffe
Readings 59; ISBN 0 255 36504 7
£12.50

Free Markets Under Siege

Cartels, Politics and Social Welfare
Richard A. Epstein
Occasional Paper 132; ISBN 0 255 36553 5
£10.00

Unshackling Accountants

D. R. Myddelton
Hobart Paper 149; ISBN 0 255 36559 4
£12.50

The Euro as Politics

Pedro Schwartz
Research Monograph 58; ISBN 0 255 36535 7
£12.50

Pricing Our Roads

Vision and Reality
Stephen Glaister & Daniel J. Graham
Research Monograph 59; ISBN 0 255 36562 4
£10.00

The Role of Business in the Modern World

Progress, Pressures, and Prospects for the Market Economy
David Henderson
Hobart Paper 150; ISBN 0 255 36548 9
£12.50

Public Service Broadcasting Without the BBC?

Alan Peacock
Occasional Paper 133; ISBN 0 255 36565 9
£10.00

The ECB and the Euro: the First Five Years

Otmar Issing
Occasional Paper 134; ISBN 0 255 36555 1
£10.00

Towards a Liberal Utopia?

Edited by Philip Booth
Hobart Paperback 32; ISBN 0 255 36563 2
£15.00

The Way Out of the Pensions Quagmire

Philip Booth & Deborah Cooper
Research Monograph 60; ISBN 0 255 36517 9
£12.50

Black Wednesday

A Re-examination of Britain's Experience in the Exchange Rate Mechanism
Alan Budd
Occasional Paper 135; ISBN 0 255 36566 7
£7.50

Crime: Economic Incentives and Social Networks
Paul Ormerod
Hobart Paper 151; ISBN 0 255 36554 3
£10.00

The Road to Serfdom *with* The Intellectuals and Socialism
Friedrich A. Hayek
Occasional Paper 136; ISBN 0 255 36576 4
£10.00

Money and Asset Prices in Boom and Bust
Tim Congdon
Hobart Paper 152; ISBN 0 255 36570 5
£10.00

The Dangers of Bus Re-regulation
and Other Perspectives on Markets in Transport
John Hibbs et al.
Occasional Paper 137; ISBN 0 255 36572 1
£10.00

The New Rural Economy
Change, Dynamism and Government Policy
Berkeley Hill et al.
Occasional Paper 138; ISBN 0 255 36546 2
£15.00

The Benefits of Tax Competition
Richard Teather
Hobart Paper 153; ISBN 0 255 36569 1
£12.50

Wheels of Fortune
Self-funding Infrastructure and the Free Market Case for a Land Tax
Fred Harrison
Hobart Paper 154; ISBN 0 255 36589 6
£12.50

Were 364 Economists All Wrong?
Edited by Philip Booth
Readings 60
ISBN-10: 0 255 36588 8; ISBN-13: 978 0 255 36588 8
£10.00

Europe After the 'No' Votes
Mapping a New Economic Path
Patrick A. Messerlin
Occasional Paper 139
ISBN-10: 0 255 36580 2; ISBN-13: 978 0 255 36580 2
£10.00

The Railways, the Market and the Government
John Hibbs et al.
Readings 61
ISBN-10: 0 255 36567 5; ISBN-13: 978 0 255 36567 3
£12.50

To order copies of currently available IEA papers, or to enquire about availability, please contact:

Gazelle
IEA orders
FREEPOST RLYS-EAHU-YSCZ
White Cross Mills
Hightown
Lancaster LA1 4XS

Tel: 01524 68765
Fax: 01524 63232
Email: sales@gazellebooks.co.uk

The IEA also offers a subscription service to its publications. For a single annual payment, currently £40.00 in the UK, you will receive every monograph the IEA publishes during the course of a year and discounts on our extensive back catalogue. For more information, please contact:

Adam Myers
Subscriptions
The Institute of Economic Affairs
2 Lord North Street
London SW1P 3LB

Tel: 020 7799 8920
Fax: 020 7799 2137
Website: www.iea.org.uk